ReShape

Emerging Church Practice
in a Volatile World

D1523190

OTHER WORKS BY MARK E. TIDSWORTH

40 Days of Prayer: Preparing Ourselves for God's Calling, 2012

Disciple Development Coaching: Christian Formation for the 21st Century, with Ircel Harrison, 2013

Shift: Three Big Moves for the 21st Century Church, 2015

Making the Shift Field Guide, 2016

Farming Church: Cultivating Adaptive Change in Congregations, 2017

^R_E**SHAPE**

Emerging Church Practice in a Volatile World

Mark E. Tidsworth

Pinnacle
LEADERSHIP ASSOCIATES

www.pinnlead.com

Copyright © 2020 Pinnacle Leadership Press

www.pinnlead.com

All rights reserved. No part of this publication may be reproduced, stored in a retrieval system or transmitted in any way by any means, electronic, mechanical, photocopy, recording or otherwise, without the prior permission of the author, except as provided by USA copyright law.

ISBN: 9798669170240

CONTENTS

Acknowledgements   1

Preface   3

This Book is a Training Log   7

Part One

Being Church in this Volatile Context   11

    Chapter 1 The Gift in Crazy Times   13

    Chapter 2 Emerging Church Practice   29

Part Two

Seven Key Practices for ReShaping Church   43

    Chapter 3 Reconnecting Church   47

    Chapter 4 Debriefing Our Experience   61

    Chapter 5 Sorting Our Progress   73

    Chapter 6 Choosing a Growth Mindset   85

    Chapter 7 Plotting Our Course   105

    Chapter 8 Aligning Our Structure   117

    Chapter 9 Launching ReShaped Church   129

Epilogue   133

Appendix One: Resources for ReShaping Transforming Church Initiative   135

Appendix Two: Church Leadership Guide for Responding to Volatile Events, English Version   137

Appendix Three: Church Leadership Guide for Responding to Volatile Events, Spanish Version   141

Appendix Four: Church Structure, St. Paul United Methodist Church   145

Endnotes   149

Acknowledgements

How large a thanks can I hand to my family? We've been sequestered here together for much of this Coronavirus pandemic and I don't know any other people on the planet I rather be with during such a volatile event. A big thank you to Sweet for giving her blessing for excessive computer time. Certainly our third-born preferred returning to college after Spring Break, yet her presence in our home was a constant source of encouragement, love, and vitality. Grammy too contributed with her humor and engagement, enriching our lives as three generations occupied our home together. Through it all we've been family with and to each other. You've helped wear off more of my rough edges with your refining mix of challenge and grace. I'm so grateful we are family.

Then the wisdom of our team at Pinnacle Leadership Associates is on nearly every page of this book. During the Coronavirus pandemic, we created new language together (Emerging Church Practice), created the ECP Webinar series together, affirmed each other when we risked new forms of ministry, and even pulled each other out of the despair ditch on occasion (whether you knew it or not). I'm grateful to the design team who read this manuscript followed by offering exceptional feedback, creating far stronger outcomes. When collective intelligence happens, it gladdens the hear in exceptional ways. Those on the Pinnacle team directly contributing to this book's formation are Ircel Harrison, Helen Hood Renew, David Brown, Doug Cushing, Debra Griffis-Woodberry, Dan Holloway, Rhonda Abbott Blevins, and Dana Seiler.

I'm very grateful too for several partners in ministry beyond Pinnacle who are making strong contributions to the formation of ReShape. Before Coronavirus times, we were already partnering with Central Seminary of Kansas City in their Thriving Congregations Initiative which is funded by The Lilly Endowment. When everything broke lose, or rather shut down, the Thriving Congregations Initiative pivoted quickly, providing support for our Emerging Church Practice Webinar Series. Currently Project Director Angie Jackson and Researcher Jessica Williams are adjusting the Thriving Congregations Initiative toward a ReShape focus. Their partnership in ministry with Pinnacle's Project Director Ircel Harrison and myself is invaluable and so appreciated.

Lastly, I'm certain this book and church process would not have emerged without our partners in ministry who are our clients at Pinnacle: clergy, church staff, churches, and denominations. At this point we've been partnering with many for fifteen years or more. Others are very new to us, having connected over a Coronavirus pandemic. For each and every one I'm more than grateful. You are such a diverse cloud of witnesses who sees fit to come together in Pinnacle activities, richly blessing us all as partners in Christ. You are a sign of the kingdom of God emerging here on planet earth. Thank you for partnering, pushing, and prodding myself and the Pinnacle Team to step toward the upward call of God in Christ Jesus.

Preface

We did the impossible in three days.

Can you remember way back in early 2020 when churches believed livestreaming their services was way beyond their technological expertise? Or what about Facebook Live? Posting worship to YouTube and sharing the link with homebound disciples seemed like a dream for many churches. We imagined online giving would take months to establish, not to mention automatic drafting from our bank accounts. Can you remember way back in early 2020 when some people believed pastors and church staff persons must work from their offices on the church property in order to be responsible and effective? Can you believe that was an expectation in some churches?

Then, the week of March 9, 2020 happened. Though the Coronavirus was spreading like wildfire through in the East, Western countries could maintain some level of denial....until then. This is the week our clergy coaching groups began the conversations. *"How can we minimize virus spread when we gather for worship? Perhaps we won't distribute paper bulletins. Maybe we will pass the peace sign rather than peace hugs or handshakes. Let's do the elbow bump rather than shaking hands."* These conversations were early in the week. By the end of that week, the conversations moved quickly like a virus to the idea of suspending in-person worship. Pastors, church staff, and lay leaders agonized over this decision. *"Gathering in our sanctuary is extremely* *comforting to all of us in our congregation. During a crisis **we need** to be together in this sacred space."* Some voices verbalized the other side of this dilemma. *"Gathering our people for in-person worship increases risk. We don't want to inadvertently harm people by gathering them for worship."* I'm estimating that first Sunday of the Coronavirus Pandemic in the United States about half of churches suspended in-person worship. After that first Sunday though, the decision to avoid exposing people to the virus clearly took precedence over worshiping in-person.

That's when we did the impossible. For years before the virus came to visit, church leaders were pushing their churches to update their systems. Online giving, online worship, online meetings...all these were innovations just waiting to happen. The benefits were obvious; yet change often needs a push. Then, in a matter of days, we accomplished what we resisted for years. Pastors and church leaders learned how to do online worship in less than a week. Churches moved nearly everything they do online. Adaptive change happened right then and there. Pastors, church staff, and lay leaders became adaptive change leaders just like that. New ways of being church emerged in the moment, meeting the need at just the right time. This is the nature of adaptive change. Conditions emerge wherein our previous ways of being church no longer suffice. To meet the challenge, we must learn and grow, adapting to our new realities. Adaptive change is required when the challenges are so different that we need a completely new set of tools than what's in our toolboxes to meet the emerging needs.

I don't know when you are reading this and how far into or beyond the Coronavirus time has taken us. At this point (June 2020) it looks like we may be in for a long siege, rather than a brief Coronavirus skirmish. Yet remember back to our extreme adaptation during those early stages. Can you remember another time when the Church at large in North America has been so responsive; so agile? Through God's creative and sustaining power, churches shifted, pivoted, learned, and broke-out in previously unimaginable ways, shifting into new forms and shapes. For those of us who regularly see the underside of church-life, keenly aware of the brokenness existing alongside the grace; seeing churches rise to the occasion and respond in such life-giving ways was so encouraging. Clearly God prepared us for moments like this, for the living of those pandemic days. When the church lays aside the inconsequential, rising to meet real life challenges with grace and strength, we are filled with joy and wonder. Thanks be to God for preparing and readying us so that we could be God's Church when the opportune time presented itself.

You might also remember the initial adrenaline rush of the Coronavirus crisis. Though the first weeks were exhausting, they were also exhilarating. We were learning, adapting, and stepping out in faith. We were like firefighters rushing into the burning building or like emergency room personnel when the patient is wheeled through the doors. Church leaders were galvanized, focused, present and accounted for. We showed up and met the need, through God's grace and strength. Yet the adrenaline rush ran its course. We human beings don't do well remaining in a constant state of high alert for weeks on end. When we do, the crash becomes inevitable. Our bodies, minds, and spirits weren't made to function in crisis mode indefinitely.

Now (June 2020), the proverbial dust is beginning to settle. The steep learning curve is leveling, allowing some breathing room. The tsunami crisis wave washed over us and is gone, leaving the ongoing choppy water with its low-level chronic stress. Since we aren't in crisis mode anymore, some people have the capacity to grow curious. There are even days when the water calms enough for us to look out ahead, wondering what's coming toward us when the tide changes. If our coaching clients are representative of the larger Church, many are beginning to ask what's next. *"What will happen on the other side of social distancing? How will we address this rising hunger for connection and community? Will our churches just go back to normal? Is finding organizational stability even realistic anymore? We are hearing so many competing expectations from the people in our church....what in the world do we do with these?"*

This is what it's like to live through volatile events with life disruption following close on its heels. Opportunities for adaptation and transformation open before us like never before. Certainly there is real and present danger as we navigate these waters. This particular volatile event may be the final life experience for some churches who were already teetering on the brink of survival. Even so, many churches are coming alive in new ways as a result of the transformation opportunities inherent in volatile events. Through the empowerment of the Holy Spirit, God's Church rises to the occasion and lives into new expressions and shapes. Watching the Church be the Church during this particular life disruption event is heartening.

Even with all the adaptation and innovation exploding in churches, I'm wondering where churches will be three months from now; six months, or a year? Will they maximize the transformation experienced during this volatile event; integrating the adaptation into their common life? Will they be stronger, more agile and flexible, able to adjust to adverse circumstances whatever they may be? In other words, will churches come out stronger and more fit than they went in? Then, what about other volatile events which come our way? This Coronavirus is the current large-scale life disruptor, yet we expect volatility to become more of the norm rather than the exception.

In no way do we want to lay aside the exceptional transformation which shows up as spiritual and organizational growth rising out of this volatile experience. Even more, as volatile experiences become more the norm, we must strengthen our adaptive muscles, developing the ability to move through whatever comes our way. Rather than simply hoping we will capture the transformation and strengthen our adaptive ability in this volatile world, we need an intentional, proactive approach. We need something more than leaving this to chance. I'm thinking we need a guided, intentional, focused, and effective process to capture and internalize the transformation we are experiencing right now. We need to partner with God, transforming our churches through these volatile life experiences, reshaping churches into greater expressions of the body of Christ.

Welcome to ReShape.

This Book is a Training Log

ReShape is a guided process for capturing and integrating the innovation and adaptation resulting from volatile life experiences, transforming churches into greater expressions of the body of Christ.

ReShape Purpose Statement

Since you have a copy in your hands, or are scrolling through these lines on your computer screen, you have made the effort to secure a copy of this book. We are therefore taking a leap, assuming that you are interested in personal spiritual formation and church transformation during or after volatile life events. Congratulations. This means you are the kind of person who looks for the spiritual growth opportunities in whatever comes your way in this life. These are the kinds of people with whom we want to partner, enjoying the companionship as together we run this race toward the upward call of God in Christ Jesus.

Given our spiritual growth aspirations, we encourage you to make this book your own. You do hereby have our blessing to scribble in it, mark it up, and otherwise personalize this book for your use. Books are not printed to remain clean and crisp, though it's gratifying to be the first one to crack one open. Books are printed so that we can use them, maximizing the growth and possibilities waiting for us in these pages. So make this book your own.

To that end, you will see two opportunities for specific responses interspersed throughout. Later we will describe at length our guiding metaphor (Body of Christ) and our guiding analogy (running the race for the upward call of God in Christ Jesus). Given these images, you will find the following two activities for your use.

Training Notes

As endurance athletes go about their training routines, they make notes when insights for strengthening their performance arise. Coaches of those athletes do the same, literally noting their observations and insights for helping their athletes. At crucial times in this book, you will be invited to step aside and reflect on your journey. You will be invited to record your observations and insights as they come to you; preserving them in the moment. At the same time, don't be constrained by these Training Notes prompts. When flashes of insight come your way, write them down in margins or the back of this book or in a journal or wherever you can. The point is to capture the transformation as it happens. Those of you participating in a ReShape small group will use your insights from your Training Notes for discussion in your small group gatherings. These will contribute to your church's transformation, so they really are important.

Body of Christ (BOC) Workouts

At the end of every chapter, you are presented with an opportunity for a workout focused on your church's transformation. These are designed to harvest the learning applicable to your specific church. Those working the ReShape Transforming Church Initiative will certainly draw on these BOC Workouts as part of their church's collective discernment. These BOC Workouts are designed with purposes beyond personal growth, contributing to the body of Christ of which you are a significant part.

By making good use of Training Notes and BOC Workouts, as well as scribbling in the margins and back pages and anywhere else in this book, you will emerge from this experience with a helpful Training Log. Your Log will describe your in-the-moment insights, personal spiritual growth, and discernment for your church's transformation.

So, I hope you are enriched by this adventure. Again, thanks for joining myself and the Pinnacle Team and may we all be reshaped into greater expressions of disciples who are the Church as we travel together.

PART ONE
BEING CHURCH IN THIS VOLATILE CONTEXT

CHAPTER ONE
THE GIFT OF CRAZY TIMES

It's funny really. For the last ten years or so, we at Pinnacle have been urging churches to adapt and transform, given the large-scale shifts in our contexts. Not only us, but every trainer, coach, writer, and consultant we know has been singing that same song. Adaptive change has been a hot topic since the early 2000s. Ronald Heifitz and Marty Linsky popularized the language of adaptive change through their book *Leadership On The Line*, published in 2002.[1] The field of adaptive change continued to expand and grow, with Alexander Grashow joining Heifitz and Linsky to publish *The Practice Of Adaptive Leadership* in 2009; a textbook for those leading adaptive change.[2] Many of us have translated their principles to leadership in church contexts, encouraging adaptation for quite some time. My book *Shift: Three Big Moves for the 21st Century Church* describes the Modern to Postmodern shift in North American culture, followed by three life-giving shifts for becoming invigorated churches; an adaptive change approach to being church.[3] *Farming Church: Cultivating Adaptive Change in Congregations* describes how to cultivate church ecosystems wherein adaptive change becomes more the norm than the exception.[4] Both of these books became Transforming Church Initiatives offered through our organization, Pinnacle Leadership Associates, occupying much of our team's vocational ministry in recent years.

This work has been fulfilling and fruitful, yet slow. It seems like those churches who could maintain their paradigms to sufficient levels, even though rapid change was occurring all around them, largely ignored or at least minimized the call to adaptation. Perhaps we human beings must feel the pinch of external circumstances before our openness to change increases enough for adaptation to happen. There's a reason for the existence of the popular and well-worn saying, "We change when the pain of staying the same exceeds the pain of changing." Either way, with the advent of the Coronavirus, the readiness quotient of churches for adaptation skyrocketed. No one has to make the case for change in these circumstances since the need for adaptation is painfully obvious. It's funny how so much progress can happen in such a short time frame when urgency is high.

The Gift of Volatile Experiences

Regardless of how we arrived here, how often is the Church handed a gift on this scale (think Coronavirus pandemic)? How often in a lifetime do we experience conditions like these which present obvious and necessary spiritual growth and church transformation opportunities? Well, the frequency of these change opportunities in the form of volatile events is changing. The frequency of contextually-driven transformation opportunities is on the rise. As we developed the content of this book and process, we initially included "Post-Coronavirus" in the title. Then we recognized the Coronavirus crisis is simply the most obvious and influential of the current volatile events coming our way. New words and acronyms appearing in our common language point to an increasingly destabilized world. "VUCA" is a concept that's been in use with specialized researchers and professionals for a long time though it seems new to many of us.

VUCA is a concept that originated with students at the U.S. Army War College to describe the volatility, uncertainty, complexity, and ambiguity of the world after the Cold War. And now, the concept is gaining new relevance to characterize the current environment and the leadership required to navigate it successfully. [5]

Our world is growing less stable as we speak; with volatility increasing. Extreme economic fluctuations, racial injustice, political destabilization, climate change...we could go on. No wonder conversations, research, and exploration of VUCA conditions is ramping up. These are some of the circumstantial or contextual large-scale shifts currently increasing in frequency and likely to continue in the near future. All of this in a culture who was already undergoing major culture change, shifting from the Modern to Postmodern Era (see my book *Shift* noted above for more on this).[6]

Though no one in their right mind *wants* volatile events to come our way more often, we recognize this trend in our common experience nevertheless. So, what do followers of Jesus do when VUCA conditions arise? How do we respond? What's our spiritual perspective or posture toward these kinds of experiences? First, we recognize we are living into the next chapter of a really good story, the big story in fact.

Framing the Story

Reshaping church does not begin with a Coronavirus Pandemic, nor with any other large or small life disruption event. Instead, we start with the big story; the story of God and this world. This big story gives shape to every smaller story ever told. This is the narrative running through the universe, turning history into salvation-history. God's creation of this universe and involvement with humankind is the frame through which we look at our experience. God's story, the most-expansive story ever, is the ongoing story in which we find ourselves.

We in this Christian Movement are part of an ongoing story whose first chapters were written before time began. Before the beginning, God was. Then God's Spirit spoke water, earth, plants, animals, and humankind into existence. Ever since, God has been taking initiative, reaching out and connecting with humankind, drawing us into God's own story. With great wonder we recognize we are part of the unfolding story of God in this world while this story is shaping us in the following ways.

This story guides and informs most everything, especially how we relate to God. Christian disciples find it very natural to explore what may be God's role in these major world crises or challenges. Since early in our story, when adversity arises, faithful people have interpreted trials and tribulations as the judgment of God (see the Old Testament). Then, perhaps God judged we human beings desperately needed help, sending God's Son into the world that we might find life even in the brokenness. Perhaps the judging on this side of heaven is done and God is working for the redemption, restoration, and renewal of humankind rather than punishing us into submission through calamity (rain falls on the just and unjust). The advent of Jesus Christ began a new age for humankind. Jesus himself described his mission and ministry as inaugurating the kingdom of God. After his resurrection, he handed off his disciples to the Holy Spirit, encouraging them to share the good news that the kingdom has come. Jesus established God's Church, serving as a sign of the kingdom's coming to earth. The Apostle Paul describes the Church as the body of Christ, no less. Amazingly, we are invited to see ourselves as the ongoing embodiment of the message and ministry of Jesus in this world. This is the message and ministry we continue even now; the good news of the gospel.

The body of Christ is our guiding metaphor for reshaping church. We are living, breathing expressions of God's Church located in communities across the world. We as the body of Christ take shape in various forms and expressions reflecting the vast diversity in the kingdom of God. Since we are living bodies, we not only come in a variety of shapes and sizes but we are also found in varying degrees of health. When we were exploring using the word reshape for this book and process, we researched its use. Who knew there were so many physical fitness programs called reshape? Despite the possibility of confusion, we decided to go forward with this title, recognizing that becoming more fit is one of our aspirations as bodies of Christ. Our hope is that churches will improve their health through intentionally cooperating with God's efforts toward reshaping them. The big story of God is the frame through which we look; giving shape to our identities. The big story of God tells us who we are; disciples of Jesus gathered into the body of Christ. Since the beginning God has been shaping and reshaping us as individual disciples and gathered bodies of Christ.

This big story of God gives us direction. As a living body (church), our calling is not to sit still, waiting for the conclusion of history. Instead God has chosen to include us in this world's remaking. It's like the Church is an endurance athlete participating in a trail race over varied terrain, pushing and straining for the prize of becoming fully formed disciples who partner with God towards the kingdom's arrival.

> *Not that I have already obtained this or have already reached the goal; but I press on to make it my own, because Christ Jesus has made me his own. Beloved, I do not consider that I have made it my own; but this one thing I do: forgetting what lies behind and straining forward to what lies ahead, I press on toward the goal for the prize of the heavenly call of God in Christ Jesus. Let those of us then who are mature be of the same mind; and if you think differently about anything, this too God will reveal to you. Only let us hold fast to what we have attained.*
>
> Philippians 3:12-16, NRSV

Since this is so, we are a work in progress. We have not arrived, not yet made the prize our own, but we strain forward to what lies ahead. Since this is so, every life experience as we run toward the prize is a spiritual growth and transformation opportunity, including volatile events. We believe that God works through every life experience to help us grow in our faith. Have you noticed how many churches have dropped the phrase "Christian Education" for the more active phrase "Christian Formation," describing their aim toward becoming more fully formed disciples? Our aim is to continue growing, becoming vessels of faith, hope, and love. A primary calling of God's Church is to form disciples, inviting us to look for the spiritual growth and transformation opportunities in every life experience.

These bodies of Christ then are bodies in motion. They are not idly and passively waiting for Christ's return. They are actively pursuing transformation, integrating the disciple and church development opportunities in every life experience along their running routes. They are intentionally participating with God's activity toward bringing the kingdom to earth as it is in heaven. While understanding ourselves as bodies of Christ is our *guiding metaphor* in ReShape, running our race for the upward call of God in Christ Jesus is our *guiding analogy*. We are bodies of Christ running our races, pursuing the upward call of God in Christ Jesus. This big story of God gives direction to our journeys.

This big story of God empowers and sustains us as we run our races. Do you remember when GPS systems first came out for use as navigational devices for vehicles? Small black plastic mounting devices were attached to windshields or dashboards. Black GPS devices, about the size of smart phones, were attached to these mounts with power cords running to the power outlets below. Since then, GPS systems have continued to evolve. Now trail runners wear GPS watches which can record not only the elapsed time during a race, but the distance and the elevation traversed. Before choosing a trail run, many runners will ask how many feet of vertical climbing they can expect on a course. Their GPS watch will record this number for them over the course of the race. Since what goes up must come down (so they say), trail runs include a variety of topographical features. Uphills, downhills, flats, and creeks are typical terrain for trail runners; including periods of extreme exertion and periods of slower running or pacing. This topographical variety in trail running reminds us of the varied terrain we experience as pilgrims travelling along life's way.

So, this big story of God gives this body of Christ who's on the move sustaining power for the race. Looking through this frame, we see ourselves as part of a bigger story, living out our church's role in the larger story of God. When the going gets tough, we remember that we are not running alone. We travel surrounded by the witness of all the saints who have gone before us and in the company of all the saints currently running, wherever on this planet they may be. When we face volatile experiences and grow weary with the wear and tear of facing extreme circumstances, we turn to the author and perfecter of our faith, casting ourselves on God. We turn to our teammates in the race, drafting off each other in turn, encouraging and supporting. God knows how to care for us and God knows how to empower us. Where human strength ends, God's empowerment begins. This big story of God empowers and sustains us during the race, no matter what the terrain.

This big story of God takes shape in local churches. Every human being is just like any other human being in most ways. Human genomes are the same in every one of us except for .001 percent.[7] We are far more alike than we are different. But though we may be nearly genetically identical, there is great variation in the personalities and life experiences between humans. No two of us are alike in our personhood, though we are very similar genetically. Our life experiences interact with our genetics and personalities to give shape to our unique ways of being human.

The same is true for churches, with each becoming its own unique expression of God's Church. Over the years of consulting with churches from many different denominations, it's clear that you can't read a book by its cover. Even within each denomination, there is great variety in the character or personhood among churches. Though churches share the same DNA and commission from God, they take shape in a rich variety of ways.

Churches, local bodies of Christ, are directly presented with transformation opportunities during and after times of volatility and life disruption. Since every life experience is a Christian formation opportunity and since every church relates to its common life in unique ways, we are called toward spiritual growth through volatile events. This is our calling, our hope, and our mission – to become more mature disciples of Jesus Christ who partner with God towards the kingdom coming to earth.

Even so, we are not the first disciples to experience major life-changing events. The New Testament writers open a door of insight into how early disciples interpreted the events of their lives. To that end, there are certain moments in time when it seems like the opportunities for spiritual growth expand, presenting themselves like gifts to be received. Since Greek was the common language when the New Testament was written, Biblical writers made use of the two common Greek words for time. First, Chronos was the Greek work for marking time as we know it, the measuring of time as it passes, regardless of its significance. Watches and clocks measure Chronos. Yet Kairos, the other Greek word, described those mystical moments when time takes on deeper meaning. Kairos describes those moments of opportune time, when something sacred and significant is appearing. Kairos is the time when something we've waited for finally arrives or when the varied strands of momentous events come together to form a beautiful pattern. It's difficult to avoid lapsing into mystical language when describing Kairos. This word appears 87 times in the New Testament, so its use in describing spiritual experiences in the Bible is prevalent.[8]

So, disciples of Jesus are constantly looking for Kairos moments as Chronos passes. We are aware that God is always working toward good in every life circumstance. We then, are looking for how God will bring good from all events, including volatile life disruption events.

Through capturing the gains from this current Coronavirus crisis, we will develop the muscles to help us be ready for whatever comes our way as churches. This kind of approach to life, one wherein we look for the spiritual growth and transformation opportunities in each life event, is not new to the Christian Church. With a keen eye, disciples of Jesus are in the habit of looking for the meaning and significance in life events. Even more, we look for how we can grow and mature as disciples through each life experience.

So many instances of innovation and transformation are rising out of extreme life disruption experiences; in our culture and in bodies of Christ. This is what we are hoping for on the other side of volatile events. In no way do we want to miss the exceptional responses of our churches when extreme circumstances come our way. This is the purpose of ReShape; capturing and integrating the growth rising out of volatile experiences, expanding our capacity for becoming adaptive, mission-congruent expressions of church.

▲ Training Notes ▲

The Big Story

Why you? Why do you participate in this Christian Movement? What is it about the big story of God that you are a disciple of Jesus Christ? I'm not asking why you participate in your church, but instead why you are involved in the Christian Faith itself. What is it about the Way of Jesus that you are a part of this spiritual movement called Christianity?

Snap-Back Danger

As we run this race for the upward call of Christ, we recognize the inherent growth opportunities along the way. When we begin emerging from crises, we recognize the danger of losing the dramatic and swift gains. We are hearing the same fear from enough church leaders now to call it a chorus of concern. They are afraid their churches will snap-back like a rubber band once this current crisis is over, regressing to their previous level of functioning, abandoning the transformation coming out of these adaptive moments. *"We are learning so much in this crazy time, but I'm afraid the desire for normalcy will drive us to double-down on our former church paradigm more than ever, resisting transformation."* They don't all say it the same way, yet statements with this same meaning are the chorus of concern rising in these moments. The danger as we emerge from crisis is to function like rubber bands, snapping-back into the exact same place we were before.

For years, I've heard the Chinese symbol for crisis combines two characters: danger and opportunity. Perhaps this illustration has been used so many times because it so perfectly captures what it's like to live through volatile events that disrupt our lives. Snapping-back to previous levels of functioning as churches is a primary danger, while capturing and integrating the transformation is the primary opportunity before us on the other side of life disruptions events. Before describing the ReShape process which addresses both of these factors, let's understand what drives this snap-back tendency.

The first influence driving the snap-back tendency is denial. In one sense, we all need some functional denial in order to hazard setting foot out the door each day. Were we consciously aware all the time of all the potential hazards in the world, we would cower in the corner, paralyzed with fear. Yet our brains are wired in such a way that we screen out most of the threats in our world, unconsciously choosing to focus elsewhere. I'm grateful for this ability, liberating us from the overwhelming anxiety that would otherwise come our way simply because we exist in this world.

On the other hand, we humans can also extend our circumstance denying abilities into unwanted territories. When the Coronavirus came to this USA, our first response was to minimize its presence. Let's face it, none of us wanted to acknowledge the presence of a pandemic in our communities. We worked to deny its reality as long as we could, with even the most fervent deniers eventually worn down by its relentless viral spread. Denial gave way to recognition.

A direct outcome of denial is underestimating the moment. We would like life disruption events to be blips on the radar screen, quickly passing by. Yet when we underestimate the moment, we also underestimate the impact, which leads to discounting the transformation opportunities therein. Our blind spots remain intact, preventing us from recognizing the growth opportunities right before us. When Kairos time appears, those in denial often miss the opportunity for spiritual and paradigmatic growth.

Often, it's only when one door closes that we are even interested in looking for the next open door. Volatile events and the resulting life disruption are real. For our churches to recognize the transformation opportunities in volatile experiences, we must recognize the truth in this statement. Life disruption is real, not imagined. Denying the reality and effects of adversity is not a strong, courageous, or even faithful response.

The second influence driving the snap-back tendency is the desire for normalcy. The desire for normalcy and familiar routines is understandable and natural. Remaining in a liminal state, experiencing discontinuous change indefinitely, is not sustainable. We start to yearn for nearly anything resembling normalcy, especially in our faith lives. Though we understand and resonate with this desire, we also recognize the danger inherent therein. If we don't address the need for centering and grounding ourselves as churches in healthy ways, we will snap-back to exactly the shape we were before this volatile experience came our way. The first ReShaping Practice in this book gives us a roadmap for addressing this danger, so we won't go in depth at this point. We will simply note that the desire for normalcy is real, making it a significant driver toward church snap-back.

The third influence driving the snap-back tendency is allowing our churches to become overwhelmed. During such large-scale life disruption events like Coronavirus, every organization is reacting and responding. Some are required to nearly reinvent themselves, radically transforming how they do what they do. Other organizations simply can't function, going dormant until the crisis is over.

As one might predict, remaining responsive over time becomes grueling. When volatile events come our way, the work-load of many increases dramatically. During the Coronavirus pandemic, new phrases appeared in our common conversations like social distancing, decision-fatigue, posttraumatic zoom disorder, virtual parishioner, hybrid church, zoom-fatigue, and deep cleaning. These emerging phrases are congruent with what we heard from church leaders; descriptive of a people and culture growing overwhelmed. Even though church leaders may be highly encouraged by the dramatic innovation and adaptation of their churches, they are also finding themselves drained and overwhelmed during volatile events.

How we related to being overwhelmed by the intense workload directly shapes the power and influence of this snap-back driver. When we recognize our experience, taking action to remedy the situation, then we are less likely to lose our adaptive capacity as churches. Then we can go with the creative flow of God's movement among us. Addressing the overwhelm resulting from too much intensity positions us to lower the influence of this factor.

The fourth influence driving the snap-back tendency is leaving our growth to chance. Maybe this one is a symptom of the first three influences combined. Some deny or underestimate the impact of the moment, therefore discounting the creative innovation rising in that moment. Others are so eager to get back to normal (were that possible) they quash innovation and growth. Still others are so burdened and heavy-laden they simply want life disruption and what it requires of us to go away. When our churches remain in this state, it's highly unlikely they will capture and integrate the transformation God wants to bring from their experience. They will likely leave it to chance, stumbling into transformation as a church, if at all.

Growing-Forward Opportunities

Right there alongside the dangers, crises bring opportunities. As I'm writing this Americans are watching and participating in protests in response to the killing of George Floyd in Minneapolis, MN. Long-standing racial injustice existing in our culture was brought to the forefront of the nation's attention through this tragic event. The protests in response sometimes turned violent, including protester and police injuries. Even so, I was brought to tears when viewing a video from Fayetteville, NC wherein police and protesters came face to face on a wide secondary road. Expecting a violent clash, everyone was surprised when the police took a knee, nearly bowing before protesters. Immediately the threat of violence dropped, tension dissipated, and the two sides mingled together with handshakes, hugs, and tears. This simple act of respect opened the door to healing and reconciliation right then and there. The participants in this experience recognized it as a Kairos moment, pursuing the transformation opportunity within those minutes on the clock.[9]

Every life circumstance is a growth opportunity, including the crises we encounter. As we look back over our life journeys, we recognize times of adversity were also when we grew and matured significantly. Though we would never wish adversity upon ourselves or others, we recognize and value the growth resulting from those difficult life seasons or experiences. We remember how the Apostle Paul called us to recognize the opportunity in volatile events.

> *Therefore, since we are justified by faith, we have peace with God through our Lord Jesus Christ, through whom we have obtained access to this grace in which we stand; and we boast in our hope of sharing the glory of God. And not only that, but we also boast in our sufferings,*

knowing that suffering produces endurance, and endurance
produces character, and character produces hope, and hope
does not disappoint us, because God's love has been poured
into our hearts through the Holy Spirit that has been given
to us. For while we were still weak, at the right time Christ
died for the ungodly.

Romans 5:1-6, NRSV

Again, the point is not to intentionally pursue adversity through volatile life experiences. Instead, we recognize adversity is part of life for every living organism on planet earth. Therefore, when volatile life events come our way, we look for the transformation opportunities therein, anticipating growth in endurance, character, and hope. Paul reminds us too that in the fullness of time (Kairos), Christ died for us. At just the right time, God weaves the disparate strands of activity in a frazzled world into beautiful works of art, including churches. When a local body of Christ grows to reflect the Lord Jesus more fully, running the race for the upward call of God, it is a beautiful thing to behold.

 BOC Workout

Snapping-Back

Looking at the four influences on the snapping-back tendency, which is more present in your church, the best you can tell from your perspective? Your answers, combined with other disciples from your church, will give a picture of the influences for snapping-back present in your church.

Rank them in descending order, 1-4. 1 = most present, 4 = least present.

_____ Denial

_____ Desire for Normalcy

_____ Overwhelmed Church

_____ Trusting to Chance

Now using the same list, go back and rank these on how they are influencing you personally.

Volatile Events

We all experience them personally and collectively. Everyone experienced the Coronavirus since it was a worldwide phenomenon. Are there other large-scale or even local volatile events that disrupted you and your church's life along the way? What about more personal volatile events? There's no pressure to share these if you are working this process in a group, yet you might list those which significantly impacted your personal journey. Though they were difficult, are you in a position to identify the personal growth you gained through them? You are invited to list those gains here to remind yourself of your growth along life's way.

CHAPTER TWO
EMERGING CHURCH PRACTICE

As you might expect, I'm the sort of person who's an early adopter; ready to try something new most anytime. The way I'm wired means that I'm game whenever an opportunity for change or experimentation presents itself. Over time I've learned this is simply my personality, formed from nature and nurture, influencing the way I see and experience this world.

That's why I'm so surprised at my growing appreciation of tradition. Well, more than tradition; the big story of God as expressed through the Christian Tradition. During this Coronavirus pandemic, even people like me who love the excitement of adaptation are struggling to keep our feet planted on the ground. Staying centered is challenging when most everything is swirling around us. The big story of God in which our faith story is located helps us stay grounded and centered. God's people have experienced everything life can possibly bring our way before. There are no completely new experiences under the sun, as the writer of Ecclesiastes reminds us.[1] I've discovered great comfort and strength in recognizing our spiritual kin of old moved through many volatile experiences as part of their life journeys, discovering God's faithfulness in the process. Now, we are doing the same. Locating ourselves, understanding where we stand in the flow of salvation-history, gives us courage and hope as we move ahead after volatile events.

In many ways, this is the ongoing call of God's Church no matter what its current situation. We look back to those who have gone before us, recognizing their witness to the creative and sustaining power of God. We look around in the present, recognizing we are the current chapter in the big story of God and God's Church. We look to the Holy Spirit, receiving guidance on what shape, form, and expression church may take given our current context. This is the ongoing call of God's Church; to discern how to be the best expression of the body of Christ we possibly can in the world in which we currently live. God's Church is taking shape in each moment followed by being reshaped the next as life continues onward.

▲ Training Notes ▲

Readiness for change...the author describes himself as nearly always ready for change, while also yearning for the security of tradition during volatile times. How would you describe yourself using these two ends of the change continuum (at this current point in time)? Ready for change or yearning for security of the familiar?

Two Early Urgent Questions During Volatile Events

When crisis hits, we don't waste much time debating what's necessary. Instead we invest our energy in doing what needs to be done. These two questions become the focus of our attention and activity:

1. What is necessary?
2. How do we respond?

When the Coronavirus pandemic arrived, requiring churches suspend in-person ministries and activities, church leaders quickly moved toward action. Intuitively they knew to shift worship to online formats. Swiftly they developed social distancing approaches to cultivating children, youth, and adults in our faith (disciple development). Right away churches formed online care groups for connecting and loving each other through the crisis. They even looked to their neighbors, continuing to express God's love through meeting community needs like sewing masks and distributing them to assisted living facilities and healthcare providers. Of course, they also looked to their institutional needs and assets, managing their facilities, personnel, and finances to the best of their ability. When crises come our way, *right away we identify what's really necessary when it comes to being church.*

Observing churches and their leaders allowed us to articulate the five essential functions of church. One could make the case for adding several others, yet these seem to be the core activities of many churches in this North American setting. These answer the first question, "What is necessary?" These five essential church functions will serve as the bone structure to which the muscles of this body of Christ attach. Those churches participating in the ReShape Transformation Initiative will emerge from this process with a ministry plan organized around these five core church functions.

Five Core Church Functions

When life disruption events occur, we decide what's important right away. Whether consciously or unconsciously; we decide. Every volatile experience disrupts our lives in its own unique way, with the Coronavirus being no exception. The voluntary nature of this life disruption event makes it stand out from many others. Just over a year before we moved to Charleston, SC (1989), Hurricane Hugo swept through with devastating effect. Everyone we met who was in the area during that horrific experience could tell harrowing and fascinating stories. Nearly all human systems that sustain life were disrupted by Hugo, interrupting food and water supply chains and even displacing people from safe shelter. Nearly everything changed with everyone responding to the crisis in very tangible ways. When they could, churches organized groups to care for their neighbors and eventually trickled back to worship.

That was Hurricane Hugo. The Coronavirus Pandemic was different in that most of our human systems which sustain life were intact. The virus was an invisible enemy stalking our streets, giving the illusion that everything was fine. Those who were using the internet before, continued right on. As time went on, many began experiencing job loss and financial hardship, yet the voluntary nature of the response to this crisis was unique and strange.

This meant that churches could continue to function, simply not in-person. Surely churches scrambled, but with more resources at hand than during a Hurricane Hugo volatile event. This uniqueness gave churches the opportunity to demonstrate what they really believe are essential or core church functions. Their responses demonstrated to the world what they believed was necessary when it comes to being church. As you might predict, many activities stopped, impossible to continue in the way they were previously done. Yet, many other activities continued on, just in a different form. The activities that churches transformed into another format so that they could continue....these are core church functions; those which churches will find a way to do when a pandemic hits.

Though not a perfect list, the following five core church functions describe where our energy went during the Coronavirus pandemic. Crises are clarifying events which pull back the curtains, revealing who we are and what we are about. As we listened to and served with clergy and lay leaders, these five church functions sorted themselves, presenting themselves to church leaders for attention. They seem consistent with how we understand most churches to function in North America. We will briefly describe each core function before using them to organize the spiritual growth and transformation rising from volatile events.

Worship
Worshiping communities...it's hard to get more primal than this. Is it possible to be a Christian church and not worship God together (in-person or online)? We would be hard pressed to find exceptions to this essential function of churches. Interestingly, some churches struggled with their perception of online worship, concerned that it may not be authentic or real, as seen in intradenominational debates about communion. Our view is that whenever and however we gather to worship, God inhabits the praises of God's people.

Disciple Development
Remember when we used to call this spiritual formation function of church "Christian education?" Then we realized the word education encouraged us to think in terms of knowledge transmission rather than life transformation. Our aim is to become mature, developed disciples of Jesus Christ. So, we use wording for this core church function which reflects our aim. Nearly every church gives energy, attention, and resources to experiences designed toward shaping persons into disciples of Jesus Christ.

Disciple Care
This was one of the areas of swift and amazing innovation by churches during the Coronavirus pandemic. Many quickly organized their

community into smaller groups who could care for each other through phone calls, drive-by visits, and online small group gatherings. Clearly, God's Church understands caring for one another, especially in times of crisis, as an essential church function. Again, we are shifting wording here, moving away from phrases like "pastoral care" and "member care," opening doors for more persons to provide care to disciples in congregations.

Serving Neighbors

Though churches tend to first consider how they can care for the disciples who are part of their church, they quickly turn toward their larger communities. Some volatile events present clear and actionable needs to which churches respond the best they can. Others, like the Coronavirus, require creative innovation since social distancing made more typical ways of caring impossible. But whether during a volatile event or not, caring for neighbors near and far is essential to being church. This includes the witness aspect of who we are, sharing the good news in word and deed. Like the writer of I John says, loving God and loving people are two sides of the same coin.[2]

Managing Assets

Way back in the day, we called this church function "administration." Since churches employ people, own property, and receive donations, they are required to manage these resources. Just like other organizations, they must observe the legalities required of every community organization. Yet, churches see this differently. We view the management of our resources as a distinctly spiritual activity. We believe God gives us these resources, asking us to function as stewards of them, managing them faithfully and effectively. We want to use these resources toward partnering with God toward the kingdom coming to earth. Every church we know has some resources to manage, recognizing this as a core function of churches.

The Human Response

The second primary question when crisis hits is "How do we respond?" As we travel through VUCA experiences, we are partially grounded and centered by making sense of our journeys. During the Coronavirus pandemic and afterwards, many attempts were made to identify the stages or phases of experience. Those with the eyes to see recognized that individuals and cultures as a whole were responding in certain ways at certain points in the journey. This kind of recognition is not new for we human beings as meaning-making creatures. We are constantly trying to make sense of what's happening around us in this evolving environment wherein we find ourselves.

To that end, there are three charts describing human responses to volatile life events proving very helpful. The first two are about human responses in general, with the third specifically about the response of churches and their leaders. The Institute for Collective Trauma and Growth, given its deep well of experience with persons experiencing trauma, extrapolated its learning to the experience of groups in its chart called Phases of Collective Trauma Response (website in notes).[3] Their view is that it takes 24-60 months for people groups to work through these phases to the "Wiser Living Phase." The second chart is called The Emotional Life Cycle of a Disaster, developed by Episcopal Relief and Development.[4] There are similarities in each of these, yet differences as well. Based on many conversations with clergy and church leaders, we developed this third chart called Church Leadership Guide – Stages of Response to Coronavirus specifically for church leaders and found in Appendix Two. We are grateful to Ruben N. Ortiz, Latino Field Coordinator, Cooperative Baptist Fellowship for translating this guide from English to Spanish, found in Appendix Three. Though specifically designed for leading through the Coronavirus pandemic, guidance is here for church leadership regardless of which volatile events churches are experiencing.

Best Church Practices Versus Emerging Church Practice

Best Practices = *"commercial or professional procedures that are accepted or prescribed as being correct or most effective."*

Google Online Dictionary

Stages or phases are helpful ways to understand how we respond to volatile events disrupting our lives. The ideas and practices of ReShape emerged from the volatile life disrupting Coronavirus pandemic. Early on, we at Pinnacle along with every pastor and church staff person, recognized that we didn't have tools in our toolbox for addressing this situation. Never in our lifetimes had churches voluntarily or involuntarily in this USA decided to suspend in-person meetings, including worship. This was new territory. Our first impulse was to research best practices for addressing large-scale life disruption events. Organizations like those producing these stages of response diagrams are already well-versed in best practices for organizations when traumatic experiences arrive. Before we could explore these best practices, our attention was drawn to the amazingly creative and innovative adaptations of churches and their leaders rising all around us. Besides, best practices emerge when an effort has been underway long enough for best practices to take shape and gain widespread acceptance. Though research may exist to guide other organizations, church practice was emerging in the moment, like just-in-time learning. We hope this gives readers insight into what we mean by "Emerging Church Practice" in this book's title. Best practices for many volatile experiences don't yet exist; emerging at just the right time and place when we need them for this journey.

Given the emerging nature of church practice during the Coronavirus Pandemic, instead of looking for experts from the academy, we turned to the rising experts in the field; the practitioners...clergy, church staff, and lay persons innovating in real churches. With the support of Central Seminary's Thriving Congregations Initiative funded by the Lilly Endowment, we were able to design and host The Emerging Church Practice Webinar Series. Due to the variety of locations and denominations of the church leaders who participated, the collaborative learning took on a satisfying richness and depth. Through this experience, we were able to learn much about the specific practices emerging from week to week.

Though we considered producing a book on these specific church practices, we recognized many were situation-specific, uniquely helpful for this particular Coronavirus volatile experience. Just as quickly as they emerged, many of these practices became irrelevant in that swiftly changing environment. Just-in-time learning experiences like webinars were more helpful than a book or other printed material which would be outdated before the ink dried. The need rising before churches was longer-term; the need to capture and integrate the transformation, strengthening their ability to adapt whenever volatile experiences come along.

This is the context in which ReShape took shape. Something larger than specific church practices was emerging. As we listened to church leaders and opened ourselves to the nudges of the Holy Spirit, it became clear that churches needed a structured and effective approach to guide their transformation.

The ReShape Transforming Church Initiative

As you are reading this, your church may be engaged in a ReShape Transforming Church Initiative. Other readers are here as interested individuals; pursuing the personal spiritual transformation resulting from volatile life experience(s) or as leaders pursuing ways to help their churches transform toward their better selves. Still other readers are involved in small groups who are using this book as their curriculum for a season, even though their church is not formally engaged in a ReShape TCI. Whatever brings you here, you are welcome and we hope ReShape will be helpful to you personally and as a church.

Now, an explanation of what ReShape is and how it can be used will help you maximize the benefits as we move along through this book.

ReShape is a guided process for capturing and integrating the innovation and adaptation resulting from volatile life experiences, transforming churches into greater expressions of the body of Christ.

ReShape Purpose Statement

For many years, we at Pinnacle Leadership Associates pursued strategic planning and then visioning processes with churches from many denominations. Recognizing the limitations of these processes given the swiftly moving culture and increasingly volatility in our context, we shifted our approach to Transforming Church Initiatives. TCIs are processes whose purpose is to cultivate, encourage, and facilitate adaptation in churches. Though strategic planning and visioning can be helpful, they are less so when the quickly changing conditions in our context require greater adaptability and flexibility. TCIs are designed to help churches discover their mission and identity, followed by relevant expression in their context. ReShape is our newest TCI, particularly focused on transformation resulting from volatile events.

Whether your church is formally engaged in this ReShape TCI or you simply want to help your church move ahead, knowing key moves in the formal process will help you make sense of this book as we travel along. These key moves are embedded in the process for churches who are part of a Community of Practice who is pursuing ReShape together. You won't see these referenced beyond the list below, yet you will know they are the structure provided for the TCI process with those churches pursuing ReShape with Pinnacle Leadership Associates. We hope seeing these may help those churches who are not involved in our process structure their own transformation.

Introducing ReShaping Church
Participation Discernment
Covenanting and Orienting Communities of Practice
Launching ReShape in Each Church
ReShape Small Groups
Discerning Our Shape
Implementing ReShape
Celebrating and Planning ReShaping Church
Sustaining ReShape – Training-The-Trainers

Anticipated Outcomes for ReShaping Church

Through our experience in serving with churches in a variety of ways over time, we are sensitized the fact that we cannot guarantee specific outcomes from transformation processes. Certainly, we believe God wants us to become transformed, growing into healthier and more fit bodies of Christ in our communities. At the same time there are too many variables and influences in play to guarantee aspirations will come to pass.

What we can say with confidence is that this process presents a great opportunity for churches to move forward toward the upward call of Christ. More specifically, we commit ourselves to partnering with churches toward emerging from ReShape as more invigorated expressions of the body of Christ on the other side of volatile life experiences. Anticipated outcomes for churches faithfully engaging and applying this ReShape process are

- Integrating the innovation gained through volatile experiences into church
- Gracefully laying aside those activities which have come to the end of their life cycle
- Greater spiritual imagination; emerging into the unfolding call of God while moving ahead

- Improving structure toward supporting mission and emerging expression of church
- Increasing vitality; more eagerly pursuing life and mission
- Strengthening adaptive capacity; positioning for innovation as needed in this changing world
- Turning toward a growth posture; looking for the spiritual and organizational transformation opportunities in every life experience
- Cultivating a culture of innovation wherein adaptive activity is blessed and reinforced
- Strengthening leadership through valuing leaders who call churches forward into their emerging expression of church

 BOC Workout

Anticipating Outcomes

We all have hopes for our church whether in a formal ReShape TCI or not. Looking at the anticipated outcomes identified in this chapter, which of them resonate with your hopes for your church? List your top two from this list below, followed by up to two more hopes you carry for your church.

<u>Top Two</u>   <u>Two More Hopes</u>

Five Core Functions of Church
Worship
Disciple Development
Disciple Care
Serving Neighbors
Managing Assets

Just to be clear right up front, no church is perfect. Like the old saying goes, *"When you find the perfect church, don't join it because you'll mess it up."* Acknowledging this reality can help us avoid becoming overly critical of our churches, expecting something close to heaven on earth. At the same time, we are always reflecting on our church's progress so that we can grow in our expression of church. To that end, which of these five functions do you believe your church did really well during the recent volatile event? Which received the least attention or lagged behind the others?

PART TWO
SEVEN KEY PRACTICES FOR RESHAPING CHURCH

Who really does the reshaping? No really, who or what does the reshaping of our churches? In our guiding analogy of running the race set before us, there are three primary participants in the race, each making its own contribution.

First and foremost, our aspiration is to invite God to be the primary influence on who we are as churches. After all, this IS God's Church. We are the body of Christ, living and active in the world, embodying Christ's message and ministry of love. This is who we are and what we are about. So, there's really no surprise when we turn to God each time we consider moves and activities as church. Christ is our head, while we are the body. We look to Christ when we need direction and when we approach decision-making; naturally so. In our guiding analogy, God is the coach, guiding and directing the runner toward running her best race.

Through time and experience, runners learn to trust their

coaches, receiving their guidance with openness and appreciation. Sometimes coaches provide reassurance and comfort, while other times coaches can be confrontational and challenging. Wise coaches know their runners, providing just what's needed at the right moment, helping runners live into their best races. Similarly, we trust God to provide the guidance we need when we are in need. God is the prime mover when it comes to ReShaping church; this is certainly our hope and aspiration.

A second influence on the athlete's performance during the race is the course itself. When I was a college distance runner, we ran a training route through the East Tennessee landscape called "Flat Nine." Perhaps I remember this route so clearly because it was aptly named, while most other routes traversed hills or even mountains. This is how the journey is for us Christ-followers; sometimes flat and easy while other times steep and difficult. The context in which we find ourselves contributes to the shape of our churches. We are incarnational people, living our faith in community contexts. The geographical features of our running routes influence how and what we do as churches. Volatile life experiences make it clear that our circumstances directly influence how churches take shape.

The third influence on how our race turns out is the runners themselves; the people who are the body of Christ. When we reflect on God's interaction with churches, we grow amazed at how much God trusts us. Though we are the body of Christ, God gives us great freedom to shape and form our collective church lives. Certainly, God provides the guidance we need, yet God gives us opportunity to be co-creators in church formation. This is the work of the church; positioning and organizing ourselves for pursuing God's mission in this world. God calls us to join in God's work of bringing the kingdom to earth as it is in heaven without prescribing every step of the journey. Instead God trusts us to recognize the clues given by the Holy Spirit while giving shape and form to our expression of church.

As we run the race for the upward call of God in Christ Jesus, churches are shaped by synergistic collaboration between God, our context, and Christian disciples. We mix it up together, so to speak, discovering our common life as churches. Each of these three influences makes a contribution to the whole; becoming something new. When church goes well, they are collaborative enterprises, emerging into beautiful expressions of the Way of Jesus.

Given this, every life experience, whether volatile or not, is an opportunity for transformation. Our aspiration is to grow into the people God is calling us to be. The mission statements of two of our denominational partners capture this aspiration well in short, pithy ways.

Making Disciples for the Transformation of the World
United Methodist Conference

Making, Equipping, and Sending Mature Disciples of Christ
The Episcopal Diocese of
Upper South Carolina

We yearn to be disciples who become mature, reflecting the excessive love of Jesus Christ our Lord. We also yearn to be part of God's world transformation mission; signaling the coming of Christ's kingdom to planet earth.

All this brings us to the journey ahead. Whatever volatile events we as individuals or as churches experience, the opportunity for spiritual and paradigmatic transformation is laid out before us. Sometimes transformation simply happens as a result of our willingness and participation. At the same time, significant and enduring spiritual transformation often requires intentionality. To that end, you and your church are invited to engage these seven key practices for ReShaping church.

CHAPTER THREE
RECONNECTING CHURCH

Here we are completing week six of social distancing during the Coronavirus Pandemic. Allow me to remind you who are in the future how wearisome social distancing became (sorry if it's still necessary). Though some of us have a higher toleration and even appreciation for being alone, the most introverted among us are missing in-person interaction with others beyond our immediate households. Yesterday, as we walked through our neighborhood, we overheard a bit of a conversation across the street. A young couple pushing a baby in a stroller was leaving a conversation with a middle-aged man at the top of his driveway. *"Sorry I stopped you to talk. I won't do that every time you walk by my house,"* he said. *"Oh it's fine, we are happy for the conversation opportunity! Thanks for that,"* was the response. There's this great upwelling of interest in connecting with people. Previously, this couple would have walked on by because the middle-aged man would not have engaged them. Now, we are all hungry for human in-person interaction!

This reminds us what runners do soon after crossing the finish line of a distance run. Though distance running is an individual sport, there's an amazing comradery that emerges when people share a difficult and stressful experience aimed at achieving a goal (making it to the finish line). I distinctly remember those cross-country team races during high school and early college. Soon after crossing the line and catching our breath, we rushed to find each other to share our race experiences. Immediately we started telling our stories, comparing our races. Reconnecting with our team after the race was one of the great joys of running races as a team.

So, it's not surprising that after life disrupter events, disciples are eager to see their church community. They want to reconnect, sharing their stories and comparing experiences. Old language for this desire to reconnect is "Christian fellowship." Since we are the body of Christ, we want to be together as one body, especially after volatile experiences.

As noted earlier, many church leaders express fear that their churches will lay aside the adaptation and innovations, snapping-back to previous ways of functioning. Church leaders worry their people will see this life disruption event as time in parentheses, like a time-out from normal life. If so, it follows that churches would abandon the innovative church practices developed during this life disruption, since a time-out really doesn't mean much. Previously we described the drivers pushing this snap-back tendency. The danger here for church leaders is to discount, ignore, or shame the deep needs in us driving our desire for what's familiar, including our strong desire to reconnect with our team. Given this normal desire for reconnecting, before pushing our churches toward spiritual growth and transformation, let's step-back and recognize the human need driving snap-back impulses.

During significant life disruption, it feels like chaos reigns. So much of what's familiar to us is blown-up, disrupting life on many levels. We as God's people deal with life as it comes, stepping-up and responding to crises, even while experiencing the ongoing discomfort of life disruption. Then, when life disruption continues over time, our longing for anything resembling normalcy escalates. We want to see familiar faces, engage familiar routines, eat at familiar restaurants, go to familiar workplaces, and so on. We want to be together as church, knowing our connection helps keep us centered.

This desire for the comfort of familiarity and connection is not simply sentimentalism. We can reach back to the groundbreaking work of Abraham Maslow and his Hierarchy of Needs.[1] Depending on the particular life disruption, there's the possibility that all five areas of need in Maslow's model are disturbed. Maslow's belief was that we must sufficiently meet the needs of lower life functions before we can move toward the higher. Certainly, during this Coronavirus pandemic, the first two levels of need, Physiological and Safety, were threatened. When these needs are threatened or unmet, our attention is focused on resolving this dilemma. We easily understand why people are not interested in strategic thinking about church when they are unsure when their next meal will come. When another's employment vanishes, that one's attention goes to securing another source of income, rather than how to live a more fulfilling life. Maslow's Hierarchy makes clear what we intuitively understand about humankind. Our basic needs deserve attention first.

The physiological and safety needs among individual disciples in any church can vary dramatically. There are those with established and secure income streams, unthreatened by life disruption. There are others who actually increase their incomes with far too much work activity due to the nature of their work. Perhaps an even larger percentage of disciples in churches are those whose income decreases or even stops during life disruption. Finances are only one way people experience physiological and safety threats, discovering they are vulnerable in many ways.

This is an opportunity for the church to care for its neighbors. Yes, we will care for the larger community around us, yet we are called to care for our own as well. During the Coronavirus pandemic we learned that Unity Presbyterian in Denver, NC established a fund wherein disciples could give their stimulus check from the government.[2] This fund was designated for service workers who lost their income, including persons who are part of that very church. Addressing the basic needs of our church includes addressing the literal needs of individual disciples who are our church. This kind of ministry, caring for our own, permeates every one of these key moves for reshaping church.

Beyond individual needs, we need our church leaders to

strategize how to address our communal needs. Are we going to survive as a church? Will we see each other again? Will our approach to worship, along with our familiar rituals survive this event? Will our small group meeting virtually find a way to be in the same room together again? These may sound like unimportant questions, yet they are very real when life disruption occurs. After raising our awareness about the real needs of our church for reconnection, then the following three activities are worth pursuing toward connecting us with what centers us as people of faith.

▲ Training Notes ▲

During the Coronavirus memes floated around the internet like, "We are all in the same boat. The Coronavirus doesn't discriminate." Then we realized we were not all in the same boat. Our life circumstances vary so widely that we may all be experiencing the same storm, but we are riding in different boats. So, perhaps everyone in your church experienced the same volatile event while individuals in your church body experienced it quite differently. If you identified three separate words to describe your experience during the volatile event, what would they be? Please list them below and unpack their meaning in the space provided.

Reconnecting with That Which Does Not Change

On the one hand, much changes during life disruption, even in very positive ways. We are grateful for the innovation and creative responses. At the same time, the speed of change can flood our systems, overwhelming our capacity. To plant our feet on solid spiritual ground, we need to reconnect with that which does not change.

I thought the timing of its publication was very interesting when I heard a review on National Public Radio of the new children's book by Rebecca Stead entitled, *The List of Things That Will Not Change* (April 2020).[3] The story is about young Bea who experiences a volatile event; her parents divorcing. One of the early activities her family did to help Bea move through this experience was to make a list of things that will not change. The first items on the list include the fact that both her parents will always love her, no matter what. Bea keeps this list in her green notebook, treasuring the knowledge that she can count on her parent's love. When we are going through life disruption experiences, identifying our list of things that will not change is so encouraging and heartening.

We, as God's people called church, are especially poised to identify a life-giving list of things which do not change. Jesus himself encouraged us to examine what's foundational in life, building our houses upon the rock rather than the sand. During life disruption we can invite our congregation into exploration about that in our faith which does not change. Even more, when the intensity of chaos is overwhelming, this is the particular role of leadership, communicating that which does not change in our faith story. There are circumstances in which we don't have the luxury of unhurried reflection, needing immediate reminders of what sustains us as communities of faith. Here's my short list of that which does not change when it comes to being church together.

Identity
We know who we are
We are disciples of Jesus Christ

Companions
We know who we are with
We are church together

Mission
We know what we are about
We are called to partner with God toward bringing the kingdom to earth
as it is in heaven

Come what may, this is my list of things which do not change.
Knowing this, we can let go of so many other aspects of our lives,
including the inconsequential aspects of church life. When we are sure
of ourselves, the need to clutch, grasp, and cling to peripheral activities
or outdated practices decreases. Knowing our identity, our companion
group, and our mission empowers us to stand firm, even when our
running route becomes treacherous. Leading our churches to identify
and affirm that which does not change empowers us to keep running
when the route grows long and tiring. Reconnecting with the essence of
our faith is like the energy bump after a stop at the aid station along the
route. We connect to our centering and energizing faith.

Reconnecting with Community

Here in the Summer of 2020, many of us are still dreaming of
the day when we can gather in-person for worship. I anticipate turning
into a charismatic Christian that first in-person service, shouting and
celebrating the day. I AM SO eager to be with our church, worshipping
in that sacred and familiar space, moving through the familiar worship
service we know and love.

There are real human needs driving our desire for the familiar. During times of great change and transition, that which is familiar is exceptionally comforting. So, our desire for normalcy in our church experience is to be expected. We need the comfort of the familiar; of our sacred spaces, worship routines, and fellowship connections. This is where church can be a source of comfort and course correcting for people, while also addressing human needs for safety and security. Churches develop their own rhythms, practices, traditions, and rituals. They become communities of faith with consistent and cohesive cultures. These ways of being church help disciples keep their feet on the ground, staying centered in an uncentered world. The familiar ways we are church together brings great comfort to us when life is disrupted in so many other ways.

The potential leadership mistake here is to steer away from the familiar, trying to capitalize on the moment of change. Doing so may drive the human desire for the familiar underground, causing it to surface again in the form of resistance to innovation. Instead, this is the opportunity to help our people be grounded; centered again in our faith traditions. So leaders, recognize the human need for familiarity during times of great change, helping your people to reconnect to those practices which center their lives. Don't lecture them about conserving change or shame them for wanting normalcy. Instead recognize these as normal desires, meeting these needs with the familiarity of our way of being church. Then we will be ready to engage the questions about growth and change. If we don't proactively address the human needs driving this snap-back tendency, we will inadvertently create great resistance to change in our churches.

The five core church functions are very helpful at this point. Leaders can look at each of these, choosing one familiar, comforting, and strengthening activity in each which to pursue. The most obvious is worship, making the decision to resume in-person worship when it's safe and advisable. Since worshipping God is so central to our church lives, we will experience so much comfort, strength, and encouragement simply from worshipping together. At the same time, we don't suggest that leaders restart everything in each of the five essential functions. Instead, choose one activity in each of the five rather than restarting your entire church programming. This will connect disciples with what's essential in church, while preserving bandwidth for integrating and expanding growth.

Reconnecting with Sabbath Rest

Remember the sabbath day, and keep it holy. Six days you shall labor and do all your work. But the seventh day is a sabbath to the Lord your God; you shall not do any work—you, your son or your daughter, your male or female slave, your livestock, or the alien resident in your towns. For in six days the Lord made heaven and earth, the sea, and all that is in them, but rested the seventh day; therefore, the Lord blessed the sabbath day and consecrated it.

Exodus 20: 8-11, NRSV

From the very beginning, God has encouraged Sabbath rest, modeling Sabbath right in the creation narrative. This idea of Sabbath is also integrated into our faith story through its inclusion in the Ten Commandments, followed by often appearing in the gospels. Jesus frequently conflicted with the religious establishment over Sabbath rules. They were interested in the technicalities of Sabbath keeping while Jesus was interested in the spirit of Sabbath. Following Jesus' lead, part of reconnecting after life disruption is making space for Sabbath rest.

During life disruption events, we are on high alert with all hands on deck. We are innovating, adapting, and serving; doing whatever it takes to address needs while moving forward. Human beings are not made to function at this extreme level, in crisis mode, indefinitely. We call them crises because they are time-limited, requiring all our life's energy and focus for brief time periods. Some life disruption events turn into chronic disruptions. They stretch on and on, requiring us to settle into the pacing stage of response. Yet, even this stage comes to an end.

For some, this is the time when they will let down and relax. When we are far enough beyond the life disruption event to let down our guards; to not be consumed by the event anymore, then some will relax. Most of us have had the experience where we ramp up during crises, functioning well, followed by crashing once the crisis is over. Don't be surprised when disciples in your church fall apart once it's safe to reconnect. The safety of their faith community may give them the security needed to let down and experience the emotions placed on the back burner when action was needed.

Fortunately, we are a people whose faith story includes Sabbath. We are actually instructed by God to practice Sabbath, recognizing we are not God with unlimited bandwidth. Actually, there are those Christians who have been calling us toward Sabbath for some time. We in the American church fell into the practice of believing that a very busy church is a very effective and successful church. *"We are a 24/7 church,"* was a statement made with the pride of accomplishment by some churches in the recent past. More recently, voices within the church like C. Christopher Smith and John Pattison in *Slow Church: Cultivating Community in the Patient Way of Jesus* are calling us to live into the commandment to honor Sabbath rest.[4] On the other side of life disruption, expect some percentage of your congregation to let down, experiencing deep fatigue. Help them find the rest they need through the spiritual discipline of Sabbath rest, a faithful part of our faith tradition.

▲ Training Notes ▲

A gift in volatile experiences is shaking up our lives. Our routines are interrupted and we have to function differently. For some, this serves as an opportunity to reflect on their lifestyles, considering changes. Sometimes, disciples discover they were so busy, maybe even for faith-based reasons, that they lost touch with themselves and God. You are invited here to take a few moments and reflect on what Sabbath rest means for you. How might your lifestyle change on the other side of volatile events to include Sabbath rest?

Connecting New Disciples

Through life disruption experiences, there are people who discover our churches and start participating. Their involvement is not the result of a program or specific initiative designed to connect them to church. Instead, they simply become involved as a result of the church being the church, doing what churches do. During this Coronavirus pandemic, many churches are connecting with new persons through online worship. There are those who have stepped away from church life who are engaging again. Some of these are the Dones who believed they were done with church, yet find themselves becoming involved again. Others have never participated in church, finding a community gathered around the Way of Jesus interesting and even compelling during these life disruption experiences.

This means that even as our churches are rejoicing in reconnecting again, we must also include those new disciples who have engaged with us during life disruption. Now is the time to include them in the celebrations and joyful worship gatherings. Now is the time to reach out to these newer disciples in love, learning their stories and forming relationships. We don't know whether they will become active and involved persons in our faith communities, yet that's not our primary motivation. Our calling is to love our neighbors, welcoming them into our community of disciples, trusting they might taste of the Lord and find that the Lord is good.

 BOC Workout

That Which Does Not Change

The author shares his list. What's your list look like? These are faith statements or truths which you can count on no matter what happens in our world. They serve to keep our spiritual, personal, and collective feet on the ground when life is chaotic. Please make your list below, anticipating sharing it with your ReShape small group so that your church can form its list of that which does not change.

CHAPTER FOUR
DEBRIEFING OUR EXPERIENCE

Have you seen those interviews after races? Sports broadcasters catch athletes soon after the race for commentary, so soon that the athletes are still out of breath, barely able to talk coherently. We don't expect much in-depth analysis or helpful reflection from these interviews. They are more like cameo appearances, giving spectators a chance to celebrate or commiserate with their favorite runners.

Post-race interviews for endurance athletes are different. Since races are much longer and the athletes tend to stay around to cheer for and socialize with other runners, interviewers don't feel so compelled to push a microphone into the athlete's faces. There's more of a comradery among the athletes, having just shared a long, arduous race together. By watching, one can see these runners know each other and share a bond. Though they are competitors on the course, the long-distance nature of these races makes for more of a bonding experience than do sprints. These runners are a community.

Because of these factors, post-race interviews with endurance athletes tend to happen after the runners have warmed-down. They are no longer breathing hard or agitated. They are calmed and ready to reflect to some degree. They are physically and emotionally beyond the immediate effects of the race; more centered or in their right minds, so to speak.

This is what this debriefing key move is like. These key moves are fluid, flowing into each other, yet they are also sequential, building on each other. When we implement the first key move of reconnecting effectively, then we are positioned for very helpful debriefing. The first key move is designed to strengthen churches through reconnecting. This helps them settle, to put their feet on the ground, centering themselves in their faith and practice. Now they are positioned to engage this second practice for ReShaping church.

Leading with Hope

And now faith, hope, and love abide, these three; and the
greatest of these is love.
I Corinthians 13:13, NRSV

Before launching our debriefing, let's reach out and touch an extremely relevant aspect of this Christian faith story – Hope. The Apostle Paul includes hope in his list of three abiding gifts in our faith journey which sustain. We currently don't understand everything about our lives nor about God's ways with us, yet faith, hope, and love guide us onward. Since we live in hope, knowing God's good work will come to completion in us in the right timing, we can live without undue anxiety or despair. When we encounter life disruption, we are sustained and endure because of Christian hope. We know the story's ending; recognizing our story ends really well.

Living lives permeated by hope allows us to engage the reality of suffering here on earth without despairing. Certainly, we grieve and hurt and agonize as we and others suffer, yet we are not overcome or destroyed because of hope's power to sustain. Hope is a necessity as we enter a time of reflection on our life disruption experience. People with hope can engage the reality of this world with courage, moving onward.

Those in our leadership training events know I love to refer to the Stockdale Paradox as an effective leadership approach for addressing challenging situations. In his book *Good to Great*, Jim Collins describes his interview with Admiral Jim Stockdale, the highest-ranking United States military officer in the "Hanoi Hilton" prisoner-of-war camp during the Vietnam War. Admiral Stockdale is credited with saving the lives of hundreds of his fellow prisoners with his unique and steadfast approach to their captivity. He lived and taught a dual approach: ruthless honesty plus unwavering hope. As opposed to many other approaches to survival in such harsh circumstances, Admiral Stockdale called is as he saw it. The conditions were as bad as they seemed. He was ruthlessly honest about the facts of their current situation as prisoners. At the very same time, Admiral Stockdale lived out an unwavering hope; a belief that he and others would eventually win out in the end. It turns out that Admiral Stockdale was the picture of hope embodied. He completely believed they would prevail in the end, regardless of the horrific conditions in the present.[1] This is a powerful leadership approach that builds tremendous credibility by speaking the truth about our situation which we all recognize, while also calling us forth toward the ultimate reality that Christ will complete the work of salvation in the end.

I share the Stockdale approach to leadership due to the need for courageous leadership coming in this second key practice for ReShaping church. Some church leaders are hesitant to describe the reality of situations, fearing they will run off participants. Others believe they are being unfaithful to God somehow if they admit the church is challenged or struggling. Though we understand how church leaders can lapse into this perspective, letting it continue is not helpful. Those of us who are in Christ have no reason to be afraid. We move ahead with faith, hope, and love; unintimidated by the temporary circumstances of this life. Empowered by Christian hope and equipped with a leadership approach like the Stockdale Paradox, we are ready to launch our second practice for reshaping church, debriefing our race.

Recognizing Life Disruption

This year, Easter Sunday was bizarre. Since we were living in social distancing conditions, churches could not gather for in-person worship as was our custom. As the awareness that in-person worship may not happen on Easter Sunday began to sink in, plenty panicked. Reacting to their shock, people said things like, *"Easter is cancelled this year."* Soon thereafter, disciples quickly realized that we cannot stop Easter from coming. The resurrection happened and continues to happen, regardless of our ability to gather for in-person worship.

So, we made it through Easter fine. Easter morning came and the resurrection of our Lord was celebrated. In this, we rejoice. Simultaneously, this year's Easter was lacking. Not gathering in-person heightened our awareness about shared meaning which comes through communal practice. When we are in-person with our church, naming and describing the resurrection of Jesus Christ....somehow the resurrection seems more real. This is the power of faith community; embodying together our truth.

Earlier in my vocational journey, I served as a therapist in a pastoral counseling center. In that role, I learned to do Critical Incident Debriefings with organizations who experienced volatile events of various kinds. Bank robberies were common calls for debriefings, along with violence in the workplace. Given we were a pastoral counseling center who was closely connected with churches in our community, we also became providers for debriefings when churches needed them. I can remember youth and their parents gathering in a church fellowship hall after a white-water rafting accident on the mission trip which took the life of one of their youth. I can remember entire congregations gathering in their sacred spaces after critical and traumatic events related to their pastors.

Through each of these experiences, I was reminded of the power of faith community. When we gather, describe our experience, naming it for what it is; then our experience becomes more real. This helps us move through that experience toward whatever is waiting for us on the other side. Being church together in this way is part of the growth process.

Even so, I'm aware of so many churches who do not engage debriefing as part of their church process. An incident of significance occurs, carrying significant emotional impact, followed by a distinct rush to move on as quickly as possible. Though we understand the impulse to move away from emotionally-charged events in church life, we (Pinnacle Leadership Associates) are also one of the organizations who is called in later to clean up the mess. The impact of these events reverberates through the church system, becoming a part of the ongoing life of the church. When a church is unwilling to process the experience, inevitably they live in a reactionary manner to that experience, always maneuvering around it somehow. The spiritual and emotional impact lives on until it's proactively addressed and moved toward closure.

So, the first move toward debriefing our race is recognizing our experience together with our church community. We give ourselves permission to reflect; stopping and describing our recent experiences. Life disruption events are real, with varied shades of meaning and significance for various disciples in a church community. Gathering to collectively talk through the experience empowers us to name it and affirm its reality. Though it may sound strange, this move is very helpful toward releasing the power of this disruption over our lives, freeing us to move forward rather than becoming stuck in the aftermath.

Before moving ahead, we must acknowledge the presence of denial mixed with any life disruption. On the one hand, denial is a helpful, adaptive activity. Have you noticed the first word out of our mouths when we receive bad news? "No." It seems we need some space between hearing the news and believing the threatening news. The word no, though not literally true, functions to cushion the blow. The adaptive function of denial is to delay the full impact of shocking news, allowing us to gather our resources for meeting the threat. On the other hand, ongoing denial typically interferes with our ability to move through life disruption toward growth and integration. When disciples in a church continue in denial, the following two outcomes are predictable.

1. Those disciples who are not practicing denial will be feel discounted by those denying the reality or significance of life disruption. Certainly we don't all experience life disruption in the same ways. During this time of social distancing, those living with two or more other people in their homes are experiencing something very different than those living alone. During this downturn in the economy, those who lost jobs are existentially at a different place than those with secure employment or income streams. Those who were already experiencing other life disruptions, followed by this Coronavirus pandemic, are in a different situation than those who came into this from stable circumstances. This variety of experiences, even regarding the same life disruptor, causes us to give an event varying levels of significance. Those in denial, who don't understand the high impact on others, will communicate off-putting messages to others. Unconsciously those denying the significance will infer that others should get over it or not be bothered by the life disruptor. Obviously, this is not helpful in faith communities.

2. Those denying the reality or significance of life disruption events will expect the church to snap-back to previous ways of functioning, missing the growth opportunities. Since they don't believe this life disruptor is a big deal, then they don't see why we shouldn't simply return to being church like we were before this volatile event. This was simply a blip on the radar screen of life, not requiring long-term adjustment on our part, so the thinking goes. When interpreting life disruption events this way, we discount the opportunities for spiritual growth and transformation inherent within them.

When church leaders intentionally invite their congregations to stop and describe their life disruption experiences as a faith community, we breathe a sigh of relief. This communal activity helps confirm our reality, reminding us the experience was real. Through the sharing and describing we realize we were all affected by this volatile event, experiencing similar (though not the same) challenges. Church leaders who live in hope are not afraid of what will happen when they invite their people to honestly describe their realities.

Naming and Claiming Our Experience

They were a divided church. They were a divided church without a pastor. I remember their interim transition well since the lessons on church process were so powerful as we worked together during their transitional year.

Before they contacted us, conflict in their church had gathered around the person of their pastor. Half the congregation was supportive of their pastor, wanting him to remain (a call system church). Half the congregation believed the pastor was hurting the church and needed to resign. Just before a business meeting with the agenda of a congregational vote on the pastor's employment, the pastor chose to resign, rather than see the church split further. This eased the tension, with the anxiety going underground.

They called a traditional kind of interim pastor who would serve in a half-time position, leading worship and visiting the sick. They also invited our organization to walk with them in a consulting role, helping them move along in their church process. We launched this work, making good progress...to a point. We came to the time when we invited disciples to engage in visioning, considering what God's calling for them as a church might be in the near future. When a church can identify a high-level vision during the interim time, then they are positioned to search for new pastoral leadership with direction.

The team with which I was working designed a fine approach to visioning, launching our effort. Yet, when we invited the church to participate in visioning, the topic at hand was nearly always derailed, digressing into talk about the previous pastor. This happened over and over until the transition team came back together with great frustration. We stepped back, considering what our experience was telling us. With reflection, prayer, and dialogue, we realized the church was telling us that it needed to address what happened regarding their previous pastor. As their consultant, I was keenly aware of how explosive opening that conversation could be. Yet this team and myself realized the apparent necessity; designing a fascinating and courageous church intervention, so to speak.

We informed the church that we recognized their need to address what happened with the previous pastor's ministry. We described a three-part one-week spiritual experience we designed for addressing this need. First, everyone in the church was invited to write a letter, addressed to the previous pastor, which they would never send. The letter included two prompts. 1. "Your ministry among us was significant and meaningful in these ways." 2. "Your ministry among us was painful and hurtful in these ways." Disciples in this church were invited during one week to write as much as they would like under each of these prompts, listing and describing their experiences.

Second, the disciples in this church were asked to pray every day of this particular week for the well-being of the previous pastor. Whatever their feelings about the previous pastor, they were asked to lift him to God in prayer, asking God to strengthen, love, and renew that pastor. (As you know, praying for someone changes us while also contributing to spiritual movement.)

Third, the disciples in this church were invited to an event in their fellowship hall at the week's end. After a meal, the church gathered in front of two tables with three paper shredders arranged on them. After a hymn and prayer (locating this experience in the context of worship), we described the format of this gathering. People were invited first to stand and read some of their responses to prompt number one from their letters. After everyone who wanted a two to three-minute opportunity shared, then people were invited to share their responses to prompt number two from their letters. There was no debating or discussing what was shared since people were simply describing their own experience, speaking their truth among these witnesses. I remember being moved to tears, listening to the heartfelt descriptions of joy and pain. I also remember being moved by the respect and dignity this band of Christ-followers extended to each other while they described their experiences.

You might guess what came next. After the sharing ran its course, with a hymn playing and in an attitude of prayer, people were invited to bring their letters to the tables, shredding them. Then we offered words of explanation and benediction. *"What we just did was not magic. We as human beings have the ability to remember what happens. Yet what we just did was what we in this Christian Movement have done for centuries. We gathered as church, witnessing our truth with the community of saints. We spoke our piece, describing our experience, while witnessing one another's stories. Now we know we have spoken our truth and it's been witnessed by our people."* Then we shredded these letters to symbolize some level of closure to this experience. *"Like our spiritual ancestors, we have engaged a ritual to help us move forward in our spiritual journeys. So now, in the future, when feelings about what happened in the past related to your previous pastor arise, remember what you did right here with your church. Remember that you spoke your truth about this. If you still need help moving on, turn to someone else who is here and ask for help in letting go."* Then we prayed and left.

Later, when we came back to visioning, nobody wanted to revisit the conflict over their previous pastor. No magic, just being church together, witnessing and debriefing each other's experience. Thanks be to God.

This story also reminds me of one denominational staff with whom we work closely. At the beginning of their staff meetings they invite each person to share their highs and lows from the week. This is a great way to catch up with each other, sharing the stories of their lives. Through this practice they are indirectly reminding themselves each week that life is a mixture of positive and negative experiences, pleasant and unpleasant, and that our faith story makes space for all life's experiences. Our understanding of God and God's ways is expansive enough to integrate every part of our running routes through life.

This is what we are inviting our churches to do as part of our debriefing experience. On the one hand, many churches grow extremely innovative during volatile events, doing ministry in ways they never dreamed possible. Tremendous growth in their church paradigm happens as a result of their responses to the clear needs they encounter. We do well to remember that Christians have celebrated the good in this world from the beginning. Throughout the Bible we are encouraged to live with gratitude, giving thanks for all the good gifts we receive along life's way.

On the other hand, our faith makes room for adversity. We can describe the painful experiences in life without fear of losing ourselves to despair because of Christian hope. We recognize that in the end love wins, receiving strength and courage to engage heartache with courage. There are those Psalms in the ancient hymnbook of our faith called lament. Reading them, one cannot escape the fact that the writer and companions are enduring extreme life disruption. Plenty Psalms of lament end on a low note, without rising again to praise. Sometimes God's people need to cry out in the presence of each other and God. Resolution is not circumstantial change, but is the peace which comes from describing our journey with God and our church.

To this point, it sounds as if recognizing our experience is only about the painful parts of life disruption. Though there is no denying pain is involved, that is only part of the story. A primary driver behind this ReShape book and church process is the desire to identify, harvest, and integrate the good growth resulting from life disruption events. As mentioned already, many churches innovated more during the first month of Coronavirus-life than they did during the previous ten years! Recognizing our experience includes describing the positive, forward-moving, and mission-congruent growth in our churches. The Stockdale Paradox gives us a way to recognize both the pain and the gains. We can realistically describe the difficulties of life disruption while also describing the growth rising-up in response to the disruption. We describe and name our highs and lows in the context of our faith communities. Identifying the gains is the work of the next key practice for ReShaping church, sorting our progress.

Another Word About Grief

Reading through the Lament Psalms, the profound grief dripping off every page is startling. These are not songs of joy or praise; rather heart-wrenching expressions of a broken-hearted community struck by loss. Our spiritual ancestors intuitively knew their need to voice their grief, finding creative mediums through which they could collectively mark and witness their pain. Because of their courageous grief expression, they moved forward to live and love and discover resurrection another day.

Even as I write this, I'm aware of my desire to move past the grief section of this book as quickly as possible. My spiritual disposition is generally the sunny, summer type, optimistic about the future. Sometimes I'm reluctant to stay with the pain long enough, giving it its due. Looking around, I'm clearly not alone. We Christ-followers love the resurrection, the Easter seasons of life. We revel in God's good gifts, eager for opportunities to celebrate. Yet deep in our spirits, we know that we must travel through the cross before resurrection comes. Our churches will do well to make space for lament, giving grief its due, like those who've gone before us. When we do, we drain off some of grief's ability to haunt us as we move along. When we don't adequately tend to our grief, it waits just out of view, looking for opportunities to ambush our collective lives as churches. We've seen enough church conflict and destructive acting-out to know that grief doesn't recede into the background gracefully. Greif requires attention, inviting the healing presence of God into our traverse through the valley of shadow.

BOC Workout

Naming and Claiming Our Experience

You are invited to write your letter, addressed to God. Since these may become part of your church's record of experiences during your volatile event, we recommend you use this format: up to one typed page length (single-spaced), with two prompts.

1. What I lost during this volatile event
2. What I gained during this volatile event

In addition to your letter, we invite you to look over the Psalms in the Old Testament. There's a wide variety of experiences described, from celebration to despair. After starting on or even completing your letter, you will likely find a Psalm which reflects the spirit of your experience. Please add the Psalm number to the bottom of your letter. Those involved in a ReShaping small group are invited to bring their letters with them to the next gathering. As always, there's no requirement to share yours. On the other hand, if you are willing, your letter will help shape your church's story of its journey during this volatile event.

CHAPTER FIVE
SORTING OUR PROGRESS

As the people were filled with expectation, and all were
questioning in their hearts concerning John, whether he
might be the Messiah, John answered all of them by saying,
"I baptize you with water; but one who is more powerful
than I is coming; I am not worthy to untie the thong of his
sandals. He will baptize you with the Holy Spirit and fire. His
winnowing fork is in his hand, to clear his threshing floor
and to gather the wheat into his granary; but the chaff he
will burn with unquenchable fire."

Luke 3:15-17, NRSV

Are you the Messiah? John the baptizer was very clear in his response. *"No!"* Instead, he points to the one who is coming and invokes a common image for those original hearers. They were familiar with threshing techniques wherein grain is separated from the inedible parts by tossing it into the air, allowing the lighter parts to drift away from the heavier grain. Then the grain is gathered from the threshing floor. There's scholarly debate about how much this analogy refers to the ultimate judgment versus to the refining process of spiritual growth through the Holy Spirit's work in our lives.[1] Here we are going with the latter interpretation.

Significant volatile events which disrupt our lives are spiritual growth opportunities, serving to refine us as disciples. At the very least, we are influenced by life disruptions, reacting to them in helpful or unhelpful ways. Even better, as we are encouraging through this ReShape transformation process, we can proactively choose to use life disruption as an opportunity for spiritual growth. It's like life disruption experiences toss our lives up into the wind, allowing a sifting process. That which is not useful or is unnecessary may fall away during challenging circumstances. That which is life-giving (like grain) remains, sustaining us as we travel along. Life disruption experiences provide the opportunity for sorting the grain from the chaff.

Life disruption events provide the opportunity for sorting valuable grain from unhelpful chaff. Choosing growth means intentionally letting go unhealthy, outdated, or irrelevant personal or church practices while taking hold of healthy, life-giving personal and church practices. May we choose growth mindsets as we run our races.

Based on this scripture, visualize a team of runners one week after their race, gathering with their coach in the conference room of their training facility. They've had time to reconnect with each other, celebrating or commiserating, depending on how each person's race unfolded. They've talked through the race a hundred times, reliving each obstacle or easy patch. They've had some time off, resting and recovering with the soreness mostly gone. Now they are ready to sort their race.

We too reconnected with our church (team), celebrated being together again, debriefed our experience and rested, positioning ourselves for recognizing the grain and the chaff. To some degree we have been sorting all along; the entire season of life disruption. Much of the sorting was done intuitively or unconsciously as needed. Now, we are ready to harvest the fruits of that labor through this proactive sorting opportunity.

Timing and Readiness

Before we launch our sorting, we need to consider the timing. Remember the Church Leader Guide introduced earlier? When we are in the first three stages of life disruption is not the time to sort our experience. We need all our focus and energy directed toward managing the crisis and our response to it when we are in the crises event. When the house is on fire is not the time to analyze which of our fire-fighting actions were the most helpful. Instead we simply respond to the fire, living in the moment. Afterwards, when sufficient safety and security is established, then we have the bandwidth to consider how we are changed through the life disruption event.

Where are you as a church now? For those reading in the near future, I hope the Coronavirus is beyond you enough that you can gather in-person as churches. If it's still not safe to gather in-person for worship, perhaps you did your debriefing outdoors or in a gymnasium type space. If the Coronavirus is still around and social distancing is required by the time you read this, I imagine people are accepting the necessity of meeting online, moving ahead in the conditions at hand. This ReShaping Church TCI doesn't require in-person large-group gatherings. They are ideal, yet not required. Like the early disciples described in the book of Acts, we approach life with flexibility and adaptability, making the most of each opportunity as it comes our way.

What this means for this third key practice is the obvious; do key practices numbers one and two first. Again, engaging them in-person is ideal, yet online is sufficient to gain the benefits when necessary.

▲ Training Notes ▲

How ready is your church to enter a time of sorting; of evaluating your spiritual growth and transformation during this volatile event? Good question. You are invited to consider this from a more personal viewpoint. How ready are you? Readiness means we are emotionally and spiritually beyond the volatile event enough that we can see the broader scope of life without undue influence from the volatile event. When we are in a crisis, everything is interpreted through that crisis. When we are beyond it, we can look more to the horizon. How ready are you for reflecting on your church's journey?

Big Three Sorting Buckets

I'm just off a coaching session with an excellent pastor of a mid-sized "First" church in a sizeable city. I know this pastor well after coaching him for quite a few years through several pastorates. He's capable, loving, kind, and enthusiastic. Yet, today he's struggling. This Coronavirus lingers on and on, interfering with vision implementation and new ministries which were about to start. Pulling back the covers on racism in America has exposed painful realities in our culture and in churches. This pastor is also new to this church; just getting established while also renovating the house in which he and his family live. I'm sparing you additional contextual changes complicating ministry in this church. So, how in the world do we know what to do as church leaders when this is the kind of story we find ourselves in? This is the point at which this third key practice can help.

Now that we have reconnected with each other to the best of our ability and have also debriefed our experience, we are ready to sort our progress. I'm hopeful the value of the first two key practices is becoming apparent. Practices one and two are designed to help us process what has happened, spiritually and emotionally. By doing so, we tend to the emotions which would otherwise exert too much influence on our vision, serving as filters which cloud our sight. Since we have processed those emotions in the presence of our church community, we are ready to turn the corner, moving into new space. Now we are ready to move to what many of us wanted to do before; to sort our experiences during the volatile event.

To do so, visualize three containers, buckets if you will, sitting before you. Each bucket is ready to receive items from your sorting. Each bucket is large enough to hold whatever you may want to place in it. Each bucket gives straightforward direction toward sifting and sorting the growth and transformation resulting from your volatile event.

The Continue Bucket
What did we start doing which may need continuing or expanding?

As we are beyond the sixth week now of the Coronavirus, I'm still amazed at the extreme innovation and adaptation of churches during this life disruption experience. Our organization initiated a series of webinars on Emerging Church Practice as a way to help church leaders do just-in-time learning. We were making it up as we went, innovating church in the moment. Though this was exhausting and an unsustainable work pace, we were also exhilarated. Holy Spirit winds were blowing, fanning the coals of dormancy, bursting into flames of adaptation. Many of us discovered church in fresh ways through the Coronavirus life disruptor.

When we are able to go back to church-as-we-have-known-it (if that's even possible), what did we start doing during the volatile event which we may want to continue? In 2015, we began consulting with several churches regarding their online presence. They recognized the potential inherent in the internet for connecting disciples and reaching others who were not connected to Christ or God's Church. Through the course of those consulting discussions, we found ourselves referring to their "Satellite Campuses." Since their people were already gathering online, meeting there to share life, we suggested they take note and establish church campuses online. Though a few courageous churches were pursuing this mission, many others simply were not yet ready.

Now, as we continue the Coronavirus social distancing, every church I know is gathering on their second campus. They have largely abandoned their first, original church campus for the second. In very short order, churches developed the infrastructure to do most everything on their second campuses. I'm curious what will happen when social distancing measures are eased. Will churches abandon the second campuses? The function of this continue bucket is to identify and gather the innovations during the life disruption experience which may need to continue. Collectively identify every innovative practice or activity and record them, placing them symbolically or literally in the continue bucket. Afterwards, you will have a bucket full of actionable innovations which your church can prayerfully consider, discerning which are given to you as part of your ongoing expression of church.

The Stop Bucket
What did we stop doing which may not need restarting?

Stopping a church activity, practice, or ritual which has been around for any length of time is far more difficult than starting something new. Church leaders know this, exercising great caution around activities to which we have grown attached. Often, they will start a replacement activity before stopping the original activity, hoping the original activity will die a natural death.

Though we often don't think this way, with reflection most of us recognize activities and practices have a lifespan. Few practices in our collective church lives are meant to last forever. They start because of a need, functioning in helpful ways for a time, followed by completing their purpose. Because they no longer meet a need or function in helpful ways is not a judgment on their validity. All this means is that activities, practices, and rituals have a lifespan, eventually going the way of all things.

Here's what we are describing. During life disruption events, churches don't function as they normally do (to make an understatement). They lay aside their normal activities and practices, responding to the crisis and adapting as they go. They also lay aside their expectations that typical activities and practices should continue during the crisis. Everyone knows life can't continue as usual.

During this unusual intermittent time, what did we stop doing that may not need restarting? Remember sifting the grain? During the volatile event, we stopped doing some activities which apparently are chaff with no need to return. In other words, what might be better left dormant? During the volatile event, what did we stop which we don't need to resurrect? Here are 3 ways to sort activities, programs, ministries, or rituals which might go in this stop bucket.

1. Purpose – When looking at your church's mission, you have to work really hard to make a case for alignment. Perhaps this helps you live into your mission....maybe. Yet, it actually seems tangential or really doesn't provide much payoff. During life

disruption events, some church practices die a natural death because they don't advance our purpose to any great extent.

2. Passion – What's the emotional response when you consider discontinuing? When you collectively breathe a sigh of relief, then it likely belongs in this stop bucket. Looking from the other direction, when you imagine restarting these again, what's the collective emotional response? When discouragement or fatigue rises, then perhaps that one belongs in the stop bucket. When passion for an activity is this low, then it was on life-support anyway.

3. Permission – If church leaders did not bring it up, no one else would ever mention it. When this is the case, then a church has been given silent permission not to restart something. When no one is asking for something nor cares to mention it, then there's not much energy for it. Traditionalism is the only motivator left when this is the case. Perhaps it has run its course, needing to go in the stop bucket.

During an Emerging Church Webinar, an associate pastor said something like, *"I love all the innovations underway in our church. We are doing amazing things in such wonderful ways. But I'm afraid when we can reconvene in-person we will be overwhelmed. We want to continue what we've started, but we can't do that and restart everything from before."* Lots of heads were shaking in agreement around the Zoom screen.

This stop bucket is so helpful to churches and their leaders because it helps them separate the chaff from the grain. There are few times in our lives when such obvious and natural opportunities to stop and start present themselves to churches. This is some of the good rising from life disruption events. After sorting items into the stop bucket, your church will have a collection of items which you may discontinue, if you discern they have served their purpose, going the way of all things.

The Explore Bucket
What else might the Holy Spirt be nudging us to do as a result of our experience?

Remember that creative energy-surge when you were responding to the initial stage of life disruption? It's amazing how God has created us to rise to the occasion, to react with energy and focus when crises come our way. The amygdala part of our brains is activated, shooting adrenaline through our systems, bringing us to high alert. Beyond this initial reaction comes another wave of energy that's even more focused, equipping us to integrate the prefrontal cortex with our emotions, leading to high creativity. Our spiritual imaginations fire and disciples engage with God and each other to do amazing things. Even our brains are wired to help us respond effectively when crisis comes our way.

We disciples look through the lens of faith, recognizing the significance of spiritual growth and transformation in moments like these. Though time by the clock continues at its usual pace, we recognize Kairos time has come; those significant moments when we clearly see God's movement in this world. This is when we are sensitized in new ways to the Holy Spirit's movement, connecting with the new thing God is doing. Throughout church history Kairos moments have appeared, often with volatile events as their catalyst.

So, this Explore Bucket provides a great opportunity for churches to let their spiritual imaginations run free. This is the time to recognize Holy Spirit nudges; to follow the energy rising in your church. If we let ourselves go, extending the innovations we placed in the Continue Bucket, where do we go? When we pray and discuss and give ourselves permission to dream, what comes to us? Looking at recent life disruption events as turning points, as opportunities to revision ourselves as churches, where do we go? The Explore Bucket is an opportunity to extend the innovation and adaptation from life disruption into ongoing church transformation. This is Kairos time when we recognize the Holy Spirit's movement among us as church, inspiring us to participate in God's mission in new ways.

 BOC Workout

Before you gather with your small group, we invite you to set aside time for individual discernment. Give yourself 30 minutes of protected time for reflecting and sorting. Though you may not need this much time, carving it out of your schedule and setting it aside will empower you to slow down and relax into this discernment opportunity.

Visualize these three buckets sitting on the floor out in front of you: Continue, Stop, and Explore. Invite God to join you in looking at these buckets. Recognize God's nearness, trusting God to do whatever is needed to help you make choices. In companionable silence, give yourself blessing to enjoy God's presence and companionship as you look at these buckets. There's no rush, since God will provide everything you need for what needs doing in this activity.

Then reflect on your church's journey during the recent volatile event. Allow your mind to flow wherever it will, noticing whatever comes to you. Use the three columns below to list anything which comes to mind, placing it in its bucket. Don't evaluate right now, but simply identify and list anything that comes to you. List as many items as come to mind, trusting God and yourself as you do so.

Continue   Stop   Explore

Now that you have items in each bucket, do some sorting. Invite God to continue actively engaging with you as you sort the items listed. You might cross some out. You might add more. Move toward identifying those items you would like to pursue further. Then rank them in priority order. List them again in their respective buckets by priority order, resulting in a list of up to 5 items in each bucket. Bring these lists to your group gathering for collective conversation and discernment.

Continue   Stop   Explore

CHAPTER SIX
CHOOSING A GROWTH MINDSET

Those who are distance athletes will remember their first competitions. Mine happened to be the mile run during my seventh-grade year. I clearly remember the mile-run time trial done on that simple dirt track behind Hayes Junior High School in St. Albans, WV. This was my first year on the junior high track team, so I was barely over the extreme soreness in my legs from those first weeks of practice. Watching us during each practice and making his notes, our coach determined which events my play to our strengths. Then coach gathered all those who appeared to be distance runners rather than sprinters or field event athletes. We were to do a time trial in the mile run. Without giving us much instruction besides the number of laps and how the start would go, we launched off the starting line with great enthusiasm and impressive speed. Predictably, many of us were dragging mid-way through the race, simply trying to keep moving to the finish line. We learned a thing or two about pacing through that first painful experience with mile-run.

All the accomplished endurance runners do it. They learn from each race, improving their performance based on the insights gained. When we listen to them debriefing races, we can hear the attention to detail and slight adjustments based on racing nuances. The most accomplished runners are always looking for ways to refine their running. For those of us running this race for the upward call of God in Christ Jesus, would we dare miss the learning opportunities along life's way?

The Call to Transformation

When we experience volatile events with their life disruption, we are faced with the question of how we will respond. At this point, I want to offer a theological viewpoint. The apostle Paul, in that beloved chapter eight of his letter to the Romans describes God's efforts on our behalf.

We know that all things work together for good for those who love God, who are called according to his purpose.
Romans 8:28, NRSV

Erroneously in my view, some Christians with a strong desire for someone to orchestrate everything in the universe, have interpreted this statement to mean that God **causes** all things. Upon reflection, many who might think this way at first, readily back away from that interpretation when recognizing there are many tragic and painful events in this world which we don't believe God wants for us and planet earth. Would we follow a God who perpetrates evil upon God's own children? Does God need our obedience so much that God would bring tragedy down on some of them in order to make others of them shape up and fly right? No, we believe God sent the Son into the world to redeem the world. Yes, God judged humankind was off track, needing great help. God judged we couldn't provide sufficient help for ourselves. God sent the Son to redeem and renew us, giving us new opportunities to live free.

Whenever we talk this way, especially in reference to life

disruption events, the theodicy issue arises. How can God be good and loving and allow tragedy to exist in this world? Sincere seekers and astute theologians have pursued answers to this question as long as the ability to communicate has been around. Still, there's not a completely satisfying answer for many of us. Evidently, we do see through a glass dimly, not fully understanding God and God's ways with our world. We live in hope of a fuller understanding when the veil between us and God is fully pulled back. In the meantime, we move ahead in faith, even a faith which includes doubt, trusting God nevertheless.

Now, on this side of the incarnation, is seems God is working through every event for redemptive purposes; encouraging spiritual growth and transformation (though that was the purpose of God's judgement in the Old Testament as well). It seems this is what God calls us to do; to join God in finding the transformation opportunities in every life event, including life disruption. Yet God doesn't force us to join in, giving us the freedom to choose how we will interpret everything which comes our way. We can choose to look for spiritual growth and renewal or we can choose death and decline. Every life experience is a Christian formation opportunity.

▲ Training Notes ▲

Theological Reflection: What do you think is God's role in volatile events? The author doesn't believe God causes them nor uses them to punish people. What's your view on God's role?

As I travel along in this Christ-following adventure, I'm consistently amazed by the privilege of choice. Think about it. We get to choose how we will interpret the events life brings our way. Even more, I'm amazed by God's excessive trust in humankind. It's like God creates us, giving us breath and life with the powers that come with bodies, spirits, and minds. God fills us with the Holy Spirit, living life with and through us. Then God sets us off on our life journey, like a parent who raises the kids well and then blesses them to fly the nest and make what they can of themselves. God trusts us to be faithful stewards of this life we are given, choosing well. Wow. Would you have designed life this way? Would you have trusted humankind with innate gifts and abilities and then given them freedom to steward everyone and everything on this planet as they see fit? Surely there must be something innately life-giving in our freedom to choose for God to give us that gift when the stakes are so high.

With this awareness, Poet Mary Oliver's question in *Summer Day* takes on a certain significance and urgency, *"Tell me, what is it you plan to do with your one wild and precious life?"* [1] Evidently, God trusts us to be faithful and effective stewards of this life we are given. When it comes down to it, we are given choice regarding most everything in life. Certainly, there are some givens, like height or skin color or the conditions into which we are born. These aspects of ourselves are simply handed to us as part of being human. Even so, we get to choose how we will respond to the givens in our lives.

> *Experience is not what happens to a man; it is what a man does with what happens to him.*
>
> Aldous Huxley[2]

Though written in outdated masculine language, this statement communicates important insights about our life-interpretation abilities. We even get to choose how we interpret what comes our way; choosing the meaning we give to each life experience, including each life disruption. Victor Frankle, who survived the concentration camps at Auschwitz became famous for crystalizing the belief that we always have a choice. Frankle was so fatigued from deprivation of basic needs that he couldn't even rise as a guard stood over him, beating him. Frankle remembered that he still could choose life regardless of his circumstances. No one could take his freedom to choose, even when he was stripped down to only a choice about his internal response to his external circumstances.[3]

▲ Training Notes ▲

Maybe you are not used to thinking this way. Maybe you assumed you have little choice over your actions or your reactions to what comes your way. The author describes a worldview in which we are granted great freedom along with great responsibility. What might it mean to you if you adopted this point of view; believing that God trusts you to do the best with what you are given, stewarding yourself, including how you interpret the events of your life? How might your approach to life shift?

Choosing Our Mindsets

For as he thinks within himself, so he is.
Proverbs 23:7, NASV

During a Making The Shift Process with a church, their insightful pastor was facilitating a discussion about the Missional Church Movement. As the group wrestled with what it means to be a missional church, confused discussion emerged about mission projects. Some believed the Missional Church Movement is opposed to mission projects, suggesting their missions committee is irrelevant and needs disbanding. This is when the insightful pastor made a comment which facilitated understanding. *"The Missional Church Movement is a mindset, a way of seeing ourselves as part of God's work in the world. It's not about methodology, but about a way of being. We are on mission with God all the time, whatever we are doing. Mission projects may be part of how we join God on mission, yet being missional is far more comprehensive than only mission projects. We ARE the church and we ARE on mission, all the time."* Becoming a missional church is changing our way of perceiving our role in this Christian Movement. It's about changing our mindsets.

This illustrates this ReShaping Church process. Those churches who maximize the growth rising from adverse and challenging experiences are those who have the eyes to see and ears to hear. They are positioned to harvest the spiritual growth resulting from their posture toward life experiences. They look at every life experience as an opportunity for spiritual growth and transformation. To be this kind of people; this kind of church, requires a certain level of maturity. Rather than buffeted by the winds, flitting here and there driven by emotional reactivity, mature churches look for how their calling to be church is emerging in every life experience.

Mindset Formation

Most of us recognize that people tend to approach life in growth-oriented ways....or not. Researcher Carol S. Dweck, through her book *Mindset: The New Psychology of Success* pulled the curtain back on how we humans grow, exploding my previously small perspectives. Discovering two primary insights through her social science research led to break-throughs for those interested in how we grow as human beings.

First, Dweck brought together various strands of research to identify "mindset beliefs." These are high level beliefs, conglomerations of many micro-beliefs, which help form a mindset; a way of viewing the world. Some beliefs about how the world works are small and fairly insignificant, not qualifying as mindset beliefs. Other beliefs influence much about how we function, serving to guide us through life. These mindset beliefs function like core values or life philosophies. They become keystone beliefs, guiding us over time. Some examples of keystone beliefs are:

This world is getting less safe
Money will make you happy
Everything happens for a reason
People cannot change
There is great hope for this world

Dweck and her research team discovered the power of these keystone beliefs through major experiments. Reading through her book I was amazed to see how they demonstrated the significant effects of our belief systems. They found that those who viewed aging as a natural and interesting time in life when new adventures can happen lived much longer than those believing older age was when life was shutting down. Her team discovered that physical fitness can improve simply by giving oneself credit for the activity levels already underway rather than writing-off oneself as incapable of exercising.

The difference in these mindsets is described as a growth versus fixed mindset. Fixed mindset beliefs tell us that our traits and characteristics are set, not changing much throughout life. For example, a person's intellect or ability to learn is set at a certain level. Thus, if one's not innately good at math, that one is very unlikely to improve math skills given innate limitations. People with growth mindset beliefs view their basic qualities as malleable; resources which can grow over time with effort and engagement. One major takeaway from Dweck's research is that people with growth mindsets tend to move through adversity with less difficulty, turning adverse experiences toward personal growth.[4]

Growth-Oriented Faith Story

Now, before going any further, one might ask why so much attention is given to choosing our mindsets. Isn't this a no-brainer? Don't all disciples of Jesus look for the spiritual growth opportunities in every life experience? Well, this is our aspiration. We want to grow as disciples through everything that comes our way. Yet, it's clear that too many of us are so caught up in the vicissitudes of our lives that we miss the Kairos moments. We do this individually and as churches. We are overwhelmed by the emotional overload or we are overburdened by the work-load. We interpret adverse circumstances as God's wrath rather than God's invitation. We give into despair rather than looking for God's sustaining power during volatile events. This is why we need to be decisive about our mindsets. There are so many influences trying to convince us to shut-down or ignore transformation opportunities that we must be determined to find God's invitation toward spiritual growth. This is also why this key practice comes after the sorting practice. We often need practice sorting the transformation rising from volatile events before we recognize our own freedom to interpret the meaning in volatile events.

I appeal to you therefore, brothers and sisters, by the
mercies of God, to present your bodies as a living sacrifice,
holy and acceptable to God, which is your spiritual worship.
Do not be conformed to this world, but be transformed by
the renewing of your minds, so that you may discern what is
the will of God—what is good and acceptable and perfect.
                                                    Romans 12:1-2, NRSV

So, every life experience is an opportunity to accept the call toward renewing our minds. Everything which comes along presents to Christ-followers a spiritual growth moment, life disruption events included. Inherent in the call to follow Christ is the call to transformation. God loves us completely as we are, yet loves us too much to leave us as we are. Through the renewing our minds, our perspectives, we discern what God wants; that which is good and acceptable and complete. This is the journey we travel, as individuals and as churches. We expect to become different as a result of engaging with God in our present life circumstances. This Way of Jesus contains within it the assumption that we are on a journey of transformation, becoming different people as we travel along life's way.

Assumption Disruption

By working through our understanding of God's role in volatile events, we are positioned to receive the gifts inherent in each one. When volatile events come along, our typical ways of understanding the world are shaken. Assumption disruption raises spiritual and theological questions. What does our faith mean when this particular volatile event comes our way? Some or even many of the assumptions we carried about how the world works don't explain our experience. What's happening is beyond the circle of our understanding. We experience assumption disruption. Some of us enter into full-blown faith crises. When enough of our assumptions are disrupted, we are given the opportunity to enter a season of faith re-formation.

Break-through races. Not every race for a runner is a break-through race. Yet, when they come along, it's like a doorway into an entirely new world flies open. This happened my first year in high school mid-way through the season. My mile run times were decent, placing me about mid-pack in the better track meets. But then our team travelled from West Virginia to Ohio for a multi-state regional meet. There were two heats for the mile run, with me drawing a spot in the slower heat. Even so, the competition far exceeded what I had experienced so far that year. As usual I finished the race mid-pack, yet my time was far faster than any race that season. Competing with such a strong field of runners elevated my racing to an entirely new level. I can still remember my disbelief when coach shared my time with me. The race seemed a little faster to me, but mostly normal. Now I had new information to consider. My time was close to the winning time in most meets before this one. This means I was capable of far more than I thought. So, what would I do with this new recognition of my running ability? Would I integrate this new understanding of myself as a runner, racing much faster in track meets to come?

This is what updating our church perception is about. When we experience spiritual growth and transformation, we must update our self-understanding as a church in order to integrate the growth. If we do not, we will unintentionally undermine our growth, seeing ourselves as less capable than we are.

Leadership coaching clients reinforced this lesson for me, reminding me how powerful our self-perceptions are. Over time, I've coached quite a few pastors who move to new churches, accepting roles with greater responsibility and opportunity. At first these pastors may feel a little like imposters. *"Do they really know my skill set? Does this church recognize this position is beyond what I've done before? Will I be able to rise to the occasion, serving effectively in this super-sized role?"* I'm glad when pastors are willing to share these doubts in coaching, since they open the door toward expanding their self-perception. What will happen if a pastor remains in this place of doubt, feeling like an imposter in someone else's role? When we live out of an outdated, small self-perception we will unintentionally undermine our own progress and effectiveness. This is the time for these pastors to recognize God's movement in their lives. God has called them to serve in positions with greater responsibility and opportunity, so evidently God believes in their abilities. This new church has recognized their gifts and has discerned this pastor is for them. The work ahead for these pastors is to update their self-perceptions, accepting they are the kind of pastors capable of serving in these expanded roles.

Many pastors use these new call opportunities to expand their self-perceptions in helpful ways, while there are other pastors who hold limiting perceptions not about themselves, but about their churches. We engaged with one church in a consulting role, recommended by their denomination due to decline. Their pastor agreed that something must be done to address their situation. Early in the consulting process, I met with this pastor, listening to his description of this church. His perception of the disciples in this church was that they would never change, not cooperating much with the transformation process we were pursuing. Listening further, it was clear to me that this pastor had written them off a long time ago, disbelieving they would ever change for the better. Through the course of this consultation it became clear to all of us involved that this pastor's ministry with this church was done. It's easy to see how such a limiting church-perception by a pastor would work to undermine church progress in so many direct and indirect ways. The way we understand ourselves as church, our church-perception, is powerful.

Updating Our Church-Perceptions

So, here's where we are in this ReShaping Church process. We just engaged in sorting church, filling our three sorting buckets. Now it's time to step back to consider what this means about us as a church. If we are a church who continues those practices, stops others, and leans into new expressions of who we are, then how does that shift our perceptions about ourselves? We need to update our church-perceptions in order to make space for our new emerging self (church); participating with God's transformation of our church. This is a primary activity for us during Kairos moments, allowing ourselves to be reshaped by the Holy Spirit.

 BOC Workout

The Body of Christ Workout for this key practice includes running four intervals. Distance runners know that intervals are relatively short bursts of speed followed by slower paced recovery intervals. We encourage you to engage each of the four intervals below, with brief moments of quiet prayer in between. Those readers involved in ReShape Small Groups will arrive at their group gatherings prepared to contribute to the group conversation led by your small group leader. These insights will ultimately contribute to the ReShaping of your church, making this BOC Workout significant.

Interval 1

Start with your real-life experiences. What were the adaptive and helpful moves your church made during the volatile event? Currently we are looking for that which your church did which was adaptive and helpful. There is intentional method in this appreciative, positive approach which will become clear as we move forward. For now, trust the process and list all the adaptive moves which come to mind. The prompt of this action is simply the word "We," with you filling in the sentence. The following are illustrative examples.

- We recognized the moment and adapted our church quickly during that volatile event
- We were able to quickly learn how to worship online, not missing a Sunday of worshipping together
- We trained so many of our people in technology use, equipping them to participate in worship and other online gatherings
- We quickly organized ourselves in care teams, reaching out to one another in love

List your church's adaptive and helpful moves:

We....

Interval 2

Consider what this may mean or say about your church. When you look at your list above, what does this say about a church who responded in this way? What does this mean about your adaptive capacity? What does this mean about your faith as a church? These are simply questions to help you get started. Don't limit yourself to these questions, but think broadly. Based on your experience during this crisis, what are you learning about your church? The prompt for this action may be, "We are a church who...." The insights you list are whatever they are. We are not looking for positives or negatives in particular, but rather the insights which rise to you as a result of observing how your church responded to the volatile event.

List insights on what this may mean about your church:
"We are a church who...."

Interval 3

Reflect on your previous church assumptions; perceptions you held about your church before this volatile event which may be outdated at this point. These assumptions may have been more true previously, while now they are less or not true about your church. By identifying them, you provide yourself and your church the opportunity to update or lay them aside. Here are examples which may help your reflection.

- Our church doesn't change, or is unwilling to change, or is very slow to change
- Our church is constrained by traditionalism, preventing innovation
- Nearly our entire congregation must be in agreement before we can make significant changes
- If we step outside our church paradigm when it comes to our church practice, then we will be like "those" churches who we don't respect
- If we step outside our paradigm, we will upset major stakeholders, and they will stop giving and participating
- If we continue a strong online presence, then most people won't return to in-person church activities or ministries
- If we do online worship, we will be selling out and dumbing-down our worship

As you can see, these statements largely function as constraining church assumptions, interfering with mission.

List outdated church assumptions:

Interval 4

Bring all four intervals together to update your church-perception. Now step back and reflect on these first three intervals. You identified what you did, what this may mean about your church, and what assumptions are no longer as true about your church. As you move ahead in the unfolding story of God as expressed through your church, what insights rise from this perception correction activity to guide you? Just like in interval 2, a helpful prompt is, "We are a church who...."

List potential new insights for updating your church-perception: "We are a church who....."

CHAPTER SEVEN
PLOTTING OUR COURSE

I hope the word "plotting" gives you pause, perhaps even sparking curiosity. For starters, plotting is an odd sounding word in its own rite. Then, plotting has at least two distinct meanings. First, navigators tasked with setting a course over land or sea or even through space act-out the meaning of this word. Then, plotting their course is what endurance trail runners do before going on a training run or especially before a big race. When running a 100-mile race, the course is not marked clearly at every point. Instead, runners obsess over maps beforehand, memorizing contour lines and geographical features so they can stay on course. They literally plot-out their course over the diverse terrain of the race. The second meaning of plotting has to do with planning and strategizing which an organization may do. Even more, there's a mischievous flavor to this word...dreaming and scheming the next moves an organization may make.

When I consider plotting our course as churches another phrase comes to mind: "co-conspirators with God." I'm not sure where I first heard this phrase, yet I find myself resonating with it. Our calling is to join God's movement in this world, partnering with God toward bringing the kingdom to earth as it is in heaven. The kingdom of God always comes with a surprising twist or slightly subversive posture. God's ways are not our ways so it shouldn't surprise us that God's reign upsets the status-quo; in really life-giving and refreshing ways. One might say that God is conspiring to set this world right by turning it upside down. Remember all those parables Jesus told which painted a picture of a different kind of existence; one in which the first will be last and the last will be first. God launched a revolution based on love by sending the Son into the world that we might know love. Given all this, plotting may be just the right word when we consider our next moves as the body of Christ pursuing our calling.

▲ Training Notes ▲

The author describes the second meaning of "plotting" in a way that makes it sound subversive to the status quo and established order of cultures and people groups. What do you make of this? Was Jesus this kind of person; one who modeled a life which threatened the existing powers? Based on your answers, what's that mean for today's church? How does this view of Jesus influence (or not) current churches? If you go with the author's view for a moment, believing Jesus called us to turn things upside down through the inauguration of the kingdom of God, what would that mean for disciples in our world?

Plotting Includes Discerning

Sometimes in our journeys toward the upward call of God in Christ Jesus the course itself brings certain topographical features to us. Major hill climbs are just ahead and there's no way around that climb. Steep downhills await us on the other side, with no way to avoid the jarring pounding of downhill running. Shady cool flat stretches alongside streams in the early morning light sooth us when the course takes us there. Oftentimes we don't choose where the course takes us (the circumstances of our lives), but take us onward it does.

On the other hand, there are those moments when we get to stand atop a pinnacle, looking into the distance with foresight. We are rested and renewed, ready to move forward toward new adventures. This is where we are in this ReShape process. Like runners who have looked back, mining their previous races for all the learning and growth to be found, we stand ready to discern the pathway ahead. Now we move into a time of discernment. Yes, we sorted the growth resulting from our last life disruption event into three buckets, yet we've not yet determined what to do with them. Yes, we updated our church-perception, recognizing our growth during our journey, yet we've not lived into the next expression of our church to date. Now we are ready to listen and discern God's calling for the race ahead. It's time to choose; to plot our course for the near future. We are using the word "discerning," recognizing the spiritual nature of this process, encouraging all involved to pray constantly for God's interaction with our churches as the reshaping takes place.

Those who have gone before us also experienced these moments of clear spiritual decision-making. There was that moment when Hebrew leader Joshua called the tribes to repentance, challenging them to choose their loyalties right then and there, recorded in Joshua 24:14-15, NRSV.

Now therefore revere the Lord, and serve him in sincerity
and in faithfulness; put away the gods that your ancestors

*served beyond the River and in Egypt, and serve the Lord.
Now if you are unwilling to serve the Lord, choose this day
whom you will serve, whether the gods your ancestors
served in the region beyond the River or the gods of the
Amorites in whose land you are living; but as for me and my
household, we will serve the Lord.*

Joshua clearly identified these moments as one of those unique turning points; a clear decision time, while also declaring his intent, whether others followed him or not.

After moving this far into the ReShape process, you have invested much. Now is the opportunity to discern and choose your next race. Churches who are working the ReShaping Church TCI have a ReShape Coordination Team in place who is guiding much of this discernment work. Their role is to collect the discernment done in small groups as we journey together, funneling it into your ReShaping Church Guide. Others who are not formally involved in a ReShaping TCI can use the template described below to channel your discernment.

*ReShape is a guided process for capturing and integrating
the innovation and adaptation resulting from volatile life
experiences, transforming churches into greater
expressions of the body of Christ.*
ReShape Purpose Statement

This is a good time to revisit the ReShape Purpose Statement. Our aspiration in this ReShaping process is to capture the good God is bringing from volatile events. In no way do we want to lose the creative adaptation and innovation as our churches adjust their shape, contextualizing in their current situation.

To that end, we are providing the ReShaping Church Guide which brings the discernment work of ReShape together into a guide for a church's ongoing common life and work. Each part of this guide is listed below with guidance for how to use each part. ReShape

Coordination Teams or other interested persons will find a template on the Pinnacle website for your use.

ReShaping Church Guide

Introduction
Two to four paragraphs describing the volatile event followed by the outcomes for your church.

Mission Mantra
Since we are this far into the ReShape process, you are positioned to step back and recognize your mission mantra. Not a formal mission statement; the mission mantra serves more like a motto or tag line. This mantra is shorthand for your church's highest aspiration. You are not encouraged to spend months or years creating this mantra, but instead step back and see what rises out of your ReShape journey. Later in this chapter we will give more specific suggestions for recognizing your mission mantra.

List of That Which Does Not Change
Directly from the first key practice of Reconnecting Church, this is your local church's list of that which endures, sustains, and guides your faith. This is a list of up to five which are your church's statement of that which does not change.

Debriefing Letters and Psalms
Those letters and the Psalms you chose during your Debriefing Experience work....they are a witness to the pain and joy you experienced during that volatile event. At this point in this ReShaping Church Guide you are encouraged to simply note that debriefing was part of your process and the letters and Psalms which describe your journey are included in a separate publication. We will provide a template for this document as well on our website.

Church-Perception

As we are transformed into more mature and robust churches, we let go of our previous assumptions about who we are while our minds are renewed; updating our perceptions of who we are as churches. In this section, we are listing two sets of church-perceptions.

Outdated Church-Perceptions
(List up to ten outdated church-perceptions)

Updated Church-Perceptions
(List up to ten updated church-perceptions)

Sorting Our Experience: Continue – Stop – Explore

During this ReShape process, churches sorted their experiences during volatile events into three groups (buckets). This resulted in a list of activities, ministries, and practices to either continue, stop, or explore. Here churches are listing the top ten items in each of these three categories. Again, those in the formal ReShape process have ReShape Coordination Teams who gathered the small group input, funneling this discernment into the top ten items in each category.

Five Core Church Functions

This too is the work to come of the ReShape Coordination Team; to sort the items from the three sorting buckets plus the organizational alignment work, into the five core functions of church. We recommend a list of no more than five items under each of the five core functions. You will keep the list of top ten items in each of the three sorting buckets, but not all of these items will make it into the five core church functions list of priorities. Preserving your top ten list form the three buckets allows you to return to them when needed in the future. For now, we limit the number of items in each core function to avoid overwhelming the capacity of churches.

Again, those involved in the formal ReShape process have a ReShape coach who will continue with them as they move into this new shape for their church. There are plenty more decisions to be made when it comes to implementation. We are not describing or prescribing those here, believing that's the ongoing unique work of each church. An exception to that approach is this suggestion that each church identify its timeline for engaging each action listed, staggering their start. Also, identifying who will provide leadership for each action listed will help gain traction.

Integrating Your ReShaping Church Guide

Our experience working with many churches across the denominational spectrum tells us we are approaching a crucial point in this journey. One of the more discouraging experiences of churches is to develop a ministry plan of some kind and then neglect or ignore it. A clear way to drain the momentum of a church is to get this far in the race, only to drop out. Anyone who's experienced this can easily identify. Fortunately, there are straightforward ways to avoid this problem through two clear steps. First, your church will be invited into committing to its journey of living into ReShaped church in the next chapter. Second, your church is invited to integrate your ReShaping Church Guide into your common life as a faith community. Two specific actions will position you to live into your ReShaping church vision.

First, Integrate your ReShaping Church Guide into the ongoing rhythm of your common church life. How? In every way you possibly can. Specifically, here is the first and foremost way to integrate your church's reshaping: make your ReShaping Church Guide part of every leadership team meeting. This means placing your ReShaping work on the agenda of every significant meeting. When your church staff gathers, your lay leadership team gathers, your ministry teams or committees gather; all of these need to engage your ReShaping Church Guide each gathering.

A very simple, yet effective method for tending to your ReShaping in these meetings is the use of these questions:

- Looking at our Five Core Church Functions (your list of aspirations under each), where have we made progress since last time we met? How will we celebrate this progress and who do we need to thank for serving in this way?
- Looking at our Five Core Church Functions, which needs action between now and next time we meet?
- Who is going to coordinate or lead these actions and what resources are needed to move this ahead?
- What else in our ReShaping of this church may need our attention at this time?

When your church leadership develops the habit of asking these four questions in each of their meetings, you will see great progress toward your collective aspirations. Certainly, it takes discipline to pursue this kind of implementation. Certainly, this requires leaders to do some pre-meeting work to narrow the focus. Yet, this is a proactive, methodical, disciplined, actionable way to help a church live into its aspirations.

Integration of your ReShaping Church Guide takes place in many other ways in addition this. Could someone in your church develop a responsive reading or litany based on your guide to include in worship periodically? There are likely people who would be delighted to serve your church in this way. Others would enjoy writing brief articles or blog posts describing the implementation of your aspirations. When we read, hear, or see the witness of fellow disciples about the movement of God through our church, we are strengthened and heartened.

Not only these, but any other way you can communicate, reinforce, advance, or integrate your ReShaping Church Guide is welcomed. As you start with these suggestions, you will discover more prompts from the Holy Spirit about living into your ReShaping.

Second, intentionally secure support and accountability toward implementation. Plenty of readers are in churches who are working with a ReShape Coach and a ReShape Community of Practice. When this is you, support and accountability are already integrated into your ReShape process. Others will need to exercise more creativity in designing their support and accountability.

By support, we mean persons and activities which will encourage you along the way. By accountability, we mean persons and activities who will raise your awareness when you veer away from implementation. Though support can become too soft and accountability can become too harsh, healthy expressions of each are necessary for nearly every significant transformation effort. Were ReShaping your church easy, we would not recommend anything about support or accountability. Since it isn't, we encourage you to proactively and intentionally secure these necessary actions in order to ensure your ReShaping process moves forward. Specifically, you might secure a ReShape Coach, or you might contact your denominational minister to explore forming an agreement for support and accountability. Widely publicizing your next ReShaping steps in your church increases accountability within the group.

 BOC Workout

Mission Mantra

Identifying your mission mantra is Holy Spirit inspired, intuitive, imaginative work. It's also the workout to which you are invited in this key practice. What we are looking for in a mission mantra is a brief, memorable way to articulate your church's highest aspiration. By brief, we mean a statement that's not even a sentence but is more of a phrase. This mantra is short enough to be remembered and repeated quite easily. This mantra captures the heart of our sense of purpose as a church. Here are a few examples we've collected along the way.

Making Christ Known in God's Community

Loving God and Loving People

Making Disciples for the Transformation of the World

Making Disciples Who Make Disciples

Loving God, Pursuing Justice, Making Peace

We invite you to spiritual discernment regarding your church's mission mantra. Listen, pray, and open yourself to any impressions God may bring to you. Record words or phrases or perhaps a complete mission mantra as you reflect. This will position you to engage your ReShape small group in mission mantra conversation.

The other obvious BOC Workout in this chapter is forming your ReShaping Church Guide. When your church is participating in the formal ReShape process, your ReShape Coordination Team will guide this aspect of your discernment. Those who are not part of a formal process should be able to complete their Guide with the instructions embedded in the text. Remember too that a template is available on the Pinnacle website at www.pinnlead.com.

CHAPTER EIGHT
ALIGNING OUR STRUCTURE

After runners reconnect with their team
After runners debrief their race
After runners sort their experience with their coaches and teammates
After runners update their self-perceptions to include recent progress
After runners and coaches bring their cumulative growth forward, they identify their hopes and dreams for the next race
Then, they update their training routines and systems in light of new racing aspirations

When it comes to endurance races, there is so much pre-planning involved! The longer the race, the more extensive the planning. Runners who do 100-mile races turn into tactical experts who gather with their team to plan for every terrain change and racing contingency. Their goal is to identify the support needed to effectively run this distance race. They plan their food intake, liquids, rest breaks, shoe changes, and nearly everything else to support a good run. Support is crucial when the goal is to run 100 miles as quickly and healthily as possible.

Now we are to that point as well in this ReShaping process. We recognize the need for adjusting our church activities and structure to support our new aspirations. The old saying *"form follows function"* gives us good guidance at this point. However, our church was organized and however it functioned before the most recent volatile event, it did not take into account the impact and growth we've experienced. Now we are ready to adjust our organization and activities so they support our church living into its emerging shape.

At this point we are positioned to bring much to bear on this key practice of alignment. We are building on our sense of community which was strengthened while reconnecting with our team. We are bringing a hopeful perspective since we engaged in collective debriefing of our experience, laying aside leftover emotional baggage. We are revisiting our five core church functions which include the items from each of the three sorting buckets. We are also bringing our expanded church-perception; recognizing we are being made new as a church even as we speak. We've covered much ground at this point; gaining such great discernment which will help us align our structure, organization, and activities.

Now it's time to revise how we do what we do. We reach back to the first key practice, reconnecting as church, reminding ourselves of that which does not change: identity, companioning, and mission. Who we are in Christ is secure since Christ has created us as, breathing life into his body (the church) which continues his mission and ministry here on planet earth. Knowing who we are, who we are with, and what we are about, gives us the security to bring a flexible attitude to our church structures. Keeping our structure the same is not what gives us safety and security as churches, though sometimes we slip into this belief. Our assurance comes from deeper realities.

We are free to practice openness, exploring what emerging church practice looks like in our contexts. Specifically, our aim with this key practice is to align the following four areas of church life with our emerging shape. All four are found in the managing assets bucket of core church functioning. Even so, let's give attention to one more positioning move before aligning our structure. Adjusting our church's posture will help us align structure effectively.

Our Spiritual Posture

Have you noticed that people carry themselves in a certain way with a natural posture toward life? I was with a pastor colleague who was showing me around the building of a church-focused financial organization when he introduced me to someone he knows well. As we were getting to know each other, this church professional gave an animated demonstration of my colleague's approach to ministry. *"Most pastors are pretty laid back in their approach to ministry, but not Rusty. Every day when he wakes up and gets ready for ministry he gets in his stance, (at this point he crouches down in a three-point football stance just before the ball is hiked) just waiting for the ball to be hiked so he can take off."* I laughed out loud right then and there since this description so accurately captured the posture of my pastor friend toward ministry.

When a church adopts a growth mindset, it sets its spiritual posture toward life and ministry. A growth mindset might be visualized as a person with arms stretched out in front of them, palms up, looking up expectantly, with legs positioned for movement. Just like individuals, churches have a posture towards the present and future. In no way do we want to be the church cowering in the corner in a fearful or defensive posture. Instead, when we choose a growth mindset, we are positioned for pursuing the upward call of God in Christ Jesus.

▲ Training Notes ▲

Before the recent volatile event, how would you describe your church's spiritual posture?

After moving to this point in the ReShape process, what's your church's current spiritual posture?

What do you make of your answers to these two questions? What's this mean about your church's readiness to move forward in reshaped mission and ministry?

Organizational Structure

There was a time when we believed more organization made for better organizations. I don't mean *being* organized, but instead I mean literally developing *more* organizational structure. We've all heard the stories of churches who nearly have one committee per active participant. The tendency to over-structure comes to churches naturally, growing out the Post-World War II organizational development approaches in this American context. We are ever grateful to the Builder generation for their strong contribution to developing sustainable organizations. They and their children became excellent at building the infrastructure which allowed small businesses in this country to grow large. Not only that, we can see their structural contribution in educational institutions and many non-profit and service organizations. Churches also benefited, with mainline and free church systems growing in organizational structure.

Since the 1990s, however, organizational development has been reversing course. Now the word "streamlining" is familiar, recognizing the need to eliminate structure which doesn't serve the mission. Churches recognized the value in this shift, pursuing greater simplicity in their organizational structure. *Simple Church*, a 2011 book by Thom Rainer and Eric Geiger advocating for minimal structure; is a prime example of this philosophical shift.[1] For those who would like an applied example, Rev. Susan Maddox, pastor of St. Paul United Methodist Church located in Saluda, SC, led her church through an organizational review which resulted in a very helpful streamlined model. The United Methodist Conference to which this church is connected gave its blessing to this organizational change resulting in streamlining their structure to only two ministry teams. After living into their new structure for nearly two years, Rev. Maddox says their people never want to go back to their previous church structure, enjoying the simplicity and functionality of this new approach. See Appendix Four for a look at this specific model.

After these philosophical swings, from less to more back to less again, perhaps we are in a season wherein we can relate to structure in a less reactionary way. Perhaps this is a time when we can use organizational structure as needed, avoiding developing too much or too little. In fact, let's step away from the need to assess how much structure our church currently has; instead focusing on the function of structure. To that end, perhaps this statement will help us:

We need organizational structure that sufficiently supports our mission, vision, and expression of church.

This brief statement says much about how we are church together. First, it tells what we DO NOT need organizational structure to do. We don't need it to give us security (that comes from Christ), becoming that which cannot change. We don't need it to become our highest priority, wherein everything we do must fit into our structure. We don't need our structure to drive who we are and what we do (tail wagging the dog), rather than our identity in Christ and calling from God as primary drivers.

On the other hand, we DO need our organizational structures to support who we are and what we are about. We need effective systems that run well over time, supporting our movement. We need ways of doing things (procedures) that are effective and healthy, growing out of knowledge about what helps organizations thrive (policies). We need small groups of people with specialized expertise to give direction to our efforts (ministry teams). We need an approved set of guidelines for doing the business of our churches while functioning well as organizations (founding and guiding documents).

Since we know how to go off the deep end with too much structure OR too little, now is a clear and present opportunity to align our structure with our mission, vision, and expression of church. At this point we have poured the items from our three sorting buckets into the five core church function buckets. The priority items in each of these five buckets are actually becoming our ReShape Ministry Plan. The next step is to align our church structures with this vision for being church.

Leadership Roles

How in the world do church leaders decide where to apply their energy and initiative? Everything looks worthy and important. Well, I guess one way to lead is in reactionary mode. Apart from the regularly scheduled events (like worship), church leaders can simply wait to see what issues or needs come across their desks each day. Instead, we want to equip our church leaders with everything they need to proactively guide our churches forward in mission and ministry. This is another area of church life wherein this ReShaping church process helps a group of people to gain direction in the swirl of volatility. Pastors, church staff persons, and lay leaders are grateful for the direction and guidance emerging from the ReShape process, giving clear focus to their leadership efforts.

Handing church leaders a ReShape ministry plan empowers them to say yes and no as needed. Without a clear ministry plan which identifies priorities for a season of church life, church leaders have to start nearly at zero with every decision. When there's not clarity about mission, vision, and church expression, leaders grasp whatever criteria they can in the moment when it comes to decision-making. Perhaps a simple example will demonstrate the benefits of a clear ReShape ministry plan.

This was a mid-sized mainline church who fell into the practice of a planning retreat at the beginning of each year. This retreat included the pastor, church staff persons, lay leadership team members, and ministry team leaders (committee chairs). During the retreat, they identified their top ten priorities as a church for the coming year. Some priorities were extensions of last year's ministry while others were completely new. After identifying the top ten, these leaders invited each person present to identify their part toward implementing these ten priorities. This was an example of shared ministry, believing every leader was responsible for advancing their church's mission and ministry.

Over time, this church recognized three outcomes of their

approach to leadership that enhanced their ministry. First, they made more progress toward living out their calling as a church by focusing their efforts on these top ten areas of church life. Second, they equipped their leadership with direction; clear guidance for making the daily decisions which come along in ministry. Leaders were able to say yes or no based on these ten priorities. Third, the conflict and tension levels in their church decreased because of the problem prevention inherent in this approach to leadership. During each year, when disciples in this church questioned why leadership was focusing on this but not that, leaders were equipped to quickly give the rational. *"This is what we identified as one of our top priorities for the year. This is where we need our leadership to focus. This is why they are not able to give major attention to other items. We need them to follow through with our church's priorities."* Clarity in their church over priorities and roles prevented much confusion about leadership activity.

ReShape is different than the above example in that the entire church identifies priorities for the next season of life together rather than only the leadership doing this work. We are approaching discernment of priorities in this way because of two core beliefs. First, we believe God speaks through all God's people. Discerning the focus of a church is done best when the full church community is invited into discernment. We strongly believe that we are collectively the body of Christ, valuing everyone's voice. Certainly, we funnel discernment to leadership to sharpen and organize our collective insights, yet we involve as many disciples from the church as possible in the creative process. Second, when we all participate in identifying priorities, all are more likely to participate in the implementation of those priorities. Together, we are church.

Property and Facilities

The opportunity in ReShape regarding this area of asset management is to intentionally align our property and facilities with our mission, vision, and expression of church. Over the last couple of years, I've walked with two churches through our Making The Shift Process who are on opposite ends of the spectrum regarding property and facilities. One is a church who sold its property and facility and now gathers for worship in rented space in another church's fellowship hall. This church is actively addressing the adaptive challenges which come with such a move. They are asking if it's necessary in their community for an established church to own property, gathering in their own worship space. They are exploring how their streamlined version of church without property maintenance concerns liberates them for greater missional engagement in their community. They are wrestling with their theology around place, sacred spaces, and being a sent church. Currently, they are opting for a minimalist approach, enjoying the freedom of rented space and greater flexibility.

The second church, as noted, is on the opposite end of this property and facilities spectrum. They own nearly a city block along with an activities building across the street; located right in the center of their city. This is a vibrant congregation, growing in number, with active ministry underway. Through their Making The Shift process they identified two very strong priorities, or callings we might say; small group ministry and missional community engagement. Now they are working to align their property and facilities with their priorities. How useful are their physical assets toward advancing their mission, vision, and expression of church is their current question?

These considerations are not small and can become overwhelming to churches. So, at this point in the ReShape process we are not recommending churches launch a large-scale property and facilities assessment that will take months or years to complete (unless that's actually needed). Instead, we are suggesting there may be ways to integrate your property and facilities more fully with your new priorities discovered through ReShape. Many churches have low-hanging fruit in this area of church life; small moves which yield major benefits. What possibilities present themselves right away when reflecting on your church's property and facilities in light of your ReShape ministry plan?

Budget

Churches are growing more creative in the wording they are using for their budgets. One Pinnacle colleague who also serves as a pastor refers to their church budget as their "Ministry Support Plan."[2] This is appealing to those who recognize the way we talk about what we do shapes what we do over time. Titles or names communicate meaning. Some churches may align their budget with their ReShape ministry plan by simply updating their language, adopting a name like Ministry Support Plan.

Even more, this is the opportunity to identify how your Ministry Support Plan might need adjusting in order to support your ReShape Ministry Plan. You have identified activities and programs to stop while also starting others. Church finances need to shift to support these changes. Certainly this takes time, but now is the time to identify the needed changes and ask the fitting group in your church to design your Ministry Support Plan alignment.

What About Previous Visioning?

There is one more area of church to life to consider when it comes to integrating your ReShape Ministry Plan. Some churches already have a vision with a ministry plan in place; the result of previous discernment work. ReShape then is an opportunity to refine and update your current vision with its ministry plan in light of volatile events and the resulting growth and direction in your church. It's very likely there are aspects of your church's vision from before the volatile event which remain very timely and relevant. Continue pursuing these. Other aspects of your vision will benefit from revision based on your recent progress and growth. Still other aspects of your vision may have become irrelevant, needing to go the way of all things. Refining your current vision based on the growth experienced recently will obviously strengthen you as a church.

▲ BOC Workout ▲

Aligning structure is the nuts and bolts part of being church. In many churches, specialized teams are those who are aware of these areas of church life while other disciples mostly rely on those teams to guide the church well. Even so, it may be that you gained insights during the volatile event which will could contribute to the alignment work of your church. Under each topic area below, you are invited to list any insights which could prove helpful for aligning your church with its ReShape aspirations.

Organizational Structure:

Leadership Roles:

Property and Facilities:

Ministry Support Plan:

CHAPTER NINE

LAUNCHING RESHAPED CHURCH

*When the days drew near for him to be taken up, he set his
face to go to Jerusalem. And he sent messengers ahead of
him. On their way they entered a village of the Samaritans
to make ready for him; but they did not receive him, because
his face was set toward Jerusalem. When his disciples James
and John saw it, they said, "Lord, do you want us to
command fire to come down from heaven and consume
them?" But he turned and rebuked them. Then they went on
to another village.*

Luke 9:51-56, NRSV

"....he set his face to go to Jerusalem." Sometimes it's amazing
how a very small phrase in scripture can carry so much meaning. After
the transfiguration, after another healing event, after foretelling his
death (again), **then** Jesus sets his face toward Jerusalem. It's like
everything in his life thus far builds to these moments and Jesus
determines to follow through, setting his intention. Regardless of what
would happen in Jerusalem, Jesus is determined to go. Regardless of the
pain and suffering ahead, Jesus can't be persuaded to change course.
Regardless of what it would mean for his disciples, Jesus sets his

intention. The Message version describes the emotional meaning of this phrase in verse 51, *"When it came close to the time for his Ascension, he gathered up his courage and steeled himself for the journey to Jerusalem. He sent messengers on ahead."* Come what may, the transfiguration helped Jesus determine his course. The race Jesus would run ran straight through Jerusalem on the way to his seat at the right hand of God. His face was set; his intention solidified. This was the upward call of God for Christ Jesus.

This sounds a little ominous as we connect this scripture with ReShaping church. Though death and resurrection are built into the rhythm of our faith, we are not suggesting you are on an ominous journey. Instead, we hope your excitement is growing since you are now stepping to the starting line. If you've done a race before, you know how the adrenaline shoots through your system, bringing you to high alert. We hope you and the others on the line are eager with anticipation. When the gun sounds, you jump off the line and into the race. These are exciting moments.

So, what does a faith community do when it's ready to launch into a new section of its race? What would be a helpful churchwide activity to launch this next phase of ReShape? For many perhaps, designing a worship experience may be the next step. Others may want to do a fellowship event of some kind, plus a worship service in a different location than your sanctuary. Still others may need to gather the church for a presentation of your ReShaping Church Guide, followed by worship and then social time. This is a time to be creative; listening to Holy Spirit nudges about what may be helpful. Whatever form your launch events takes, here are the purposes we are about in launching.

- We want to celebrate our church's discernment and work during this ReShaping process
- We want to celebrate God's presence and guidance which resulted in our ReShaping Church Guide
- We want to gather ourselves around our common aspirations, overtly committing ourselves to living into our emerging church shape

- We want to engage those who were not part of the ReShape process, yet are part of our church, including them in our ongoing common life and collective aspirations

Beyond churchwide launching events, how ready are we personally to move forward? Now is the time to ready ourselves for personal participation in the ReShaping of our church. The following activity is a combined workout: Training Notes (personal transformation) plus BOC Workout (collective transformation). Personal readiness contributes to the whole, while collective movement by our church contributes to personal readiness.

Training Notes & BOC Workout

Jesus' intention was set. When have you had an experience like this; one wherein you KNEW you were being called to a specific mission, move, action? How do you know when God is calling you in this way? People are put together differently....how do YOU KNOW when God's guidance shows up for you?

How ready are you for ReShaping your church? We've been on a lengthy and significant journey together. Your church has been preparing all along. What about you? How ready are you to participate in your church's ReShaping? If there are obstacles in your way, what's your strategy for addressing them? Don't overlook personal obstacles like resentment toward another disciple or unwillingness to forgive someone who's hurt you. ReShaping church is a spiritual process. We need to be in the best personal spiritual shape we can be in order to participate well with our church.

Epilogue

ReShape is a guided process for capturing and integrating the innovation and adaptation resulting from volatile life experiences, transforming churches into greater expressions of the body of Christ.

ReShape Purpose Statement

...*"into greater expressions of the body of Christ."* Like those endurance athletes driven on with purpose over varied terrain, we press on toward the goal for the prize of the heavenly call of God in Christ Jesus. Ever evolving, growing, emerging, maturing...there's something inside us that drives us onward; the yearning to become greater reflections of Jesus Christ our Lord. Since we are the body of Christ, we are a living, breathing, moving organism, yet we are incomplete on this side of heaven. We are pursuing our best expression of church to date; yearning to live into God's hopes and dreams for us. We have not yet arrived and the ReShaping of our church goes on. Our hope is that we will embody Jesus Christ in our world more clearly tomorrow than we are today. Our churches are always works in progress, bodies on the move, expressing what it looks like to be church in ever emerging ways.

And for this journey of transformation, we give thanks. This is what it is to live; to be caught up in the adventure of Jesus. Like those two dusty travelers on the Emmaus Road, may our hearts burn within us due to our nearness to Jesus the Christ as we run this race. Amen.

Appendix One
ReShape Resources

There are many ways to engage the ReShaping of your church. Here we will describe those of which we are aware, recognizing others will rise-up and take shape as ReShape moves along. First, you may want to get acquainted with our outfit if don't already know Pinnacle Leadership Associates. We've been serving the needs of clergy, church staff, churches, and denominations since 2008 through coaching, training, consulting, publishing, and web design. Browsing our website is a great way to learn more at www.pinnlead.com. Beyond this introduction to Pinnacle, here are ways churches might engage ReShape.

- Reading the book together as a leadership team or entire congregation. When you need 5 or more copies, contact us directly since we can secure them at a lower cost than retail.
- Using ReShape as your small group curriculum. The BOC Workouts and Training Notes in the text can provide the content for small groups. If you want more training in leading small groups, watch for the ReShape Small Group Leadership Guide coming soon from Pinnacle Leadership Press.
- Securing a ReShape Coach and engaging the ReShaping Church TCI. Contact us at Pinnacle to explore this possibility.
- Joining a Community of Practice (a group of 4 churches) who collectively pursue the ReShaping Church TCI. Communities of Practice are churches who share some kind of affinity; like location, size, theological viewpoint, or pastors who know each other. This is a great way to pursue transformation since the synergy of the COP moves everyone along.
- Joining a Community of Practice organized and partially funded by your denomination. Pinnacle partners with denominations to bring transformation processes to their churches, strengthening their churches and the denomination in the process. Contact your denomination to inquire about this option.
- Joining a Community of Practice with grant funding. We are currently involved in a Thriving Congregations Initiative through

Central Seminary in Kansas City which is funded by The Lilly Endowment. Other grant proposals including ReShape as their program are under consideration. Contact us to explore these options.

Certainly more approaches to engaging ReShape will rise as life moves along. We are eager to watch the innovation as it emerges.

Please feel free to contact us at: Pinnacle Leadership Associates, www.pinnlead.com, markt@pinnlead.com. We look forward to hearing from you.

Appendix Two
Church Leadership Guide for Responding to Volatile Events, English Version

An Emerging Church Practice Resource

Mark Tidsworth, Team Leader, Pinnacle Leadership Associates

Stage	On The Ground Conditions	Emotional Experience	Spiritual & Congregational Needs	Primary Leadership Activities	Pastoral & Lay Leadership Styles
First Stage -Lap 1	Suspending In Person Gatherings	Shock, Fleeting Denial, Adrenaline Rush, High Alert, Excitement	Direction & Guidance, Action, Adaptation, Innovation, Assurance	Guiding, Directing, Calling To Action, Presence, Positioning, High Activity	More Directive, Command Center Operations
Second Stage -Laps 2-3	Living In Social Distancing	Fatigue, Sadness, Longing For Community, Discouragement, Frustration	Theological Hope, Perseverance, Endurance, Sustaining Strength, Sabbath Rest & Renewal, Accepting Discomfort, Companionship, Basic Needs	Faith-Story Connecting, Call To Hope, Permission & Blessing to Rest, Confidence, Listening Coordination Basic Needs Ministry	Less Directive, More Collaborative, Pacing Collaboratively With Lay Leaders
Third Stage -Lap 4	Easing Social Distancing & Reengaging	Fatigue, Stressed, Eagerness, Excitement, Joy, Relief	Community Connecting, Celebrating, Worship & Essential Rituals, Continued Awareness and Basic Needs	Timing Discernment, Risk Assessment, Faith-Story Connecting, Shifting Church Practice, Direction & Guiding	More Directive, Focused Decisioning With Lay Leaders
Fourth Stage -Post-Race Debrief	Lifting Social Distancing With An Eye On Tracking The Virus	Joy, Relief, Sadness, Depression, Anger, Hunger For Normalcy	Comfort of Normalcy Through Ritual, Rest & Renewal, Spiritual Centering & Strengthening, Reflection, Integration, Basic Needs	Risk Assessment, Faith-Story Connecting, Facilitating Reflection-Sorting-Reshaping, Leading Process for Emerging Church Practice	Less Directive, Spiritual Guides, Process Facilitators

Church Leadership Guide: Stages Of Response To Coronavirus

In recent weeks, we have walked with many pastors, churches, and denominations as they respond to this Coronavirus Pandemic. From our vantage point, clearly there is much variety in responses and in the stages of response. Through listening closely and engaging conversations with church leaders, perspective is rising, resulting in this chart. The purpose of this chart is to help church leaders align their activity with the stages of the experience and the needs of their congregations. We hope it will help you lead your church to live into its best self during this Coronavirus Pandemic.

Guiding Analogy – Like Running a Mile Race On The Track, 4 Full Laps

Explanation of the guiding analogy will be helpful. Before track and field converted its distances to meters, the mile run was four complete laps on the track. Runners learned to the rhythm of this particular race, making strategic moves. These rhythms are useful in describing what our experience and how we can lead effectively.

Lap 1 – When the gun fires, runners jump off the line with bursts of adrenaline fueled energy, sprinting ahead to establish position. They couldn't run at this swift pace the entire race, yet do so for much of the first lap before settling into their ongoing pace. This lap involved great excitement, high energy output, and exciting maneuvering.

Lap 2-3 – This stage is the longest stage in the race. The runners settle into their pace, while also starting to feel the discomfort of oxygyn deprivation. Their adrenaline is gone, breathing hard, persevering with hope. They are working hard and uncomfortable, yet they know this won't last forever.

Lap 4 – Though fatigued and depleted, the runners accelerate with their final kick, leaving everything out on the track. There are strategic moves to make, starting their sprint at just the right moment. Their thinking and judgment can be fuzzy, since they have been exerting for so long. There is great relief in crossing the finish line.

Post-Race Debriefing – Every skilled coach pursues opportunities to debrief after races. This is when runners are settled enough to reflect on their experience, identifying the positive and negatives, considering what to integrate from the experience.

Uses of this Church Leadership Guide

Whatever stage we are in, having a roadmap for the journey is comforting. Maps also give us direction for planning our next turns. We encourage pastors in all size churches to discuss this Church Leadership Guide with church staff and lay leaders, aligning your leadership with the apparent needs in your church. No roadmap is totally accurate, so adjust this one as needed.

Guía para el Liderazgo Eclesial: Etapas en Respuesta al Coronavirus - Recurso práctico para la iglesia

Por - Mark Tidsworth, Líder de Equipo, Pinnacle Leadership Associates

Etapa	Condiciones en el terreno	Experiencia Emocional	Necesidades Espirituales y Congregacionales	Actividades en el Liderazgo Primario	Estilos de Liderazgo para la pastoral y el laicado
Primera 1ra vuelta	Suspensión de reuniones en persona.	Conmoción, negación fugaz, alta adrenalina, estado de alerta y alta emoción.	Dirección y orientación, acción, adaptación, innovación, certezas.	Guiando, dirigiendo, llamando a la acción. Mantener presencia, posicionarse, alta actividad.	Más directivo, tipo centro de comando y operaciones.
Segunda 2-3 Vuelta	Vivir en distancia social.	Fatiga, tristeza, anhelar la comunidad, desaliento, frustración.	Esperanza teológica, perseverancia, resistencia, Sostenimiento, reposo y renovación, aceptar las molestias, compañerismo y sostenimiento en necesidades básicas.	Conectando historias de fe, llamado a la esperanza, dar permiso y bendición para descansar. Confianza, ministerio de escuchar y dar respuesta a necesidades básicas.	Menos directivo, más colaborativo, en ritmo y colaboración con los líderes laicos.
Tercera 4ta vuelta	Relajando el distanciamiento social y volviendo a reunirnos físicamente.	Fatiga, stress, afán, emoción exaltada, alegría, alivio.	Conexión comunitaria, celebrando adoración y rituales esenciales, alta conciencia en necesidades básicas	Discernimiento en cuanto a tiempo, evaluación de riesgos, conectar testimonios de fe, dirección, guía y práctica para el cambio.	Más directivo, enfocado en tomar decisiones junto al laicado.
Cuarta vuelta y análisis de carrera.	Levantar el distanciamiento social con actitud vigilante ante el virus.	Alegría, alivio, tristeza, depresión, ira, deseos de normalidad.	Vuelta a la comodidad y normalidad a través de retomar los ritmos, descanso y renovación, fortalecimiento y espiritualidad centrada. Reflexión, integración, necesidades básicas resueltas.	Evaluación de riesgos, conectar testimonios de fe, facilitar la reflexión. Proceso de liderazgo para nuevas practicas de ser iglesia	Menos directivo, guía espiritual, facilitador de procesos.

Guía de liderazgo de la iglesia: etapas de respuesta al coronavirus

En las últimas semanas, hemos caminado con muchos pastores, iglesias y denominaciones mientras responden a esta pandemia de coronavirus. Desde nuestro punto de vista, claramente hay mucha variedad en las respuestas y en las etapas de respuesta. Al escuchar atentamente y entablar conversaciones con los líderes eclesiales ha crecido nuestra perspectiva sobre el asunto y como resultado hemos confeccionado esta tabla. Su propósito es ayudar a los líderes de la iglesia a alinear sus actividad con las etapas de la experiencia y las necesidades de sus congregaciones. Esperamos que te ayude a llevar a tu iglesia a vivir en su mejor momento durante esta pandemia de coronavirus.

Analogía guía: como correr una carrera de una milla en 4 vueltas completas a una pista.

Explicar la analogía será útil. Antes de que en el deporte de pista y campo se convirtieran las distancias a metros, la carrera de una milla se componía de cuatro vueltas completas en la pista. Los corredores aprendieron al ritmo de esta carrera particular de forma estratégica. Esos ritmos son útiles para describir lo que es nuestra experiencia en estos momentos y cómo podemos liderar efectivamente.

Vuelta 1: Cuando suena el disparo los corredores básicamente saltan de la línea con estallidos de energía alimentada con gran adrenalina corriendo adelante para establecer su posición. No van a correr a este mismo ritmo rápido durante toda la carrera, pero lo harán durante gran parte de la carrera. En la primera vuelta antes de establecer un ritmo continuo implicará mucha emoción, mucha energía comenzando por una buena salida.

Vuelta 2-3: Esta etapa es la más larga de la carrera. Los corredores se acomodan a su ritmo, mientras comienzan a sentir la incomodidad de la falta de oxígeno. La adrenalina va descendiendo, respiran con más dificultad pero perseveran con esperanza. Se esfuerzan, aunque sienten la incomodidad, pero saben que esto no durará para siempre.

Vuelta 4: Aunque cansados y agotados, los corredores aceleran con zancadas finales. Dejan todo en la pista. Hay movimientos estratégicos que hacer, comenzando con un buen *"sprint"* en el momento justo. El pensamiento y el juicio pueden ser confusos, porque están agotados. Entonces se da un gran alivio, cruzar la línea de meta.

En el informe posterior a la carrera todos los entrenadores expertos buscan oportunidades para informar después de las carreras. Ahí es cuando los corredores están lo suficientemente asentados como para reflexionar sobre su experiencia, identificando lo positivo y lo negativo, considerando qué integrar desde la experiencia.

Usos de esta Guía de Liderazgo de la Iglesia

En cualquier etapa en la que nos encontremos, alivia tener una hoja de ruta para el viaje. Los mapas también nos dan dirección para planificar nuestros próximos giros. Alentamos a los pastores en iglesias de todos los tamaños a discutir esto con el liderazgo de la iglesia. Trabaje con el personal de la iglesia y los líderes laicos, alinie su liderazgo con las necesidades actuales en su iglesia. Ninguna hoja de ruta es totalmente precisa, así que ajuste esta según sea necesario.

Appendix Four
Church Structure
St. Paul United Methodist Church
Saluda, South Carolina

Church Structure
St. Paul UMC, Saluda
2019

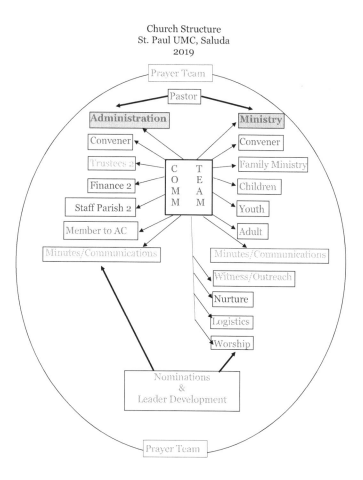

Notes

• The two conveners serve as liaisons to the congregation, represent the laity at baptisms and when new members join, etc. The administrative team convener signs charge conference papers as the church council chair. The ministry team convener is the conference and district point to contact, a role previously filled by the lay leader.

• Conveners and minute-takers do not make/second motions or vote.

• A quorum for meetings is those present and voting.

• Tenure in office for all leaders: One year, renewable up to three years.

• When there is a change in the team convener, one person (either convener or communications) carries over as a non-voting "historian" from the previous year.

• Not included in the flow chart (UMW, UMM, Alternate to Annual Conference). Representatives from these ministries could be included if they are a vital part of the leadership in a given year.

• Decisions are made through consensus rather than with a vote in order to promote unity and allow all points of view to be heard.

As a result of the Forward Focus process, St. Paul UMC formed a task group consisting of four persons, the pastor, and our congregational specialist to create a new leadership structure that would support a more streamlined decision-making process. The resulting structure consists of a ministry team, an administrative team, and a nominating committee. The ministry team meets monthly and focuses on living out our mission and vision through the various ministries of the church. The administrative team meets monthly to handle any business of the trustees, staff/parish relations, and finance areas of the church. This new structure has cut down on the number of meetings needed to make decisions and has enabled us to spend more time and energy on planning and doing ministry. Each leader is encouraged to incorporate as many people as possible in their area of ministry through the use of short-term "task groups". These groups are formed for a specific event/process/length of time and then disbanded. We have found people are much more willing to commit to a specific project for a certain length of time than to commit to a 3-year term on a committee. All of our leaders have commented that they prefer this structure and do not want to return to the traditional structure that was used prior to this year.

ENDNOTES

Chapter One – The Gift in Crazy Times

1. Ronald A. Heifetz and Marty Linsky, *Leadership on The Line: Staying Alive through the Dangers of Leading* (Boston: Harvard Business School Press, 2002).
2. Ronald Heifetz, Alexander Groshow, and Marty Linsky, *The Practice of Adaptive Leadership: Tools and Tactics for Changing Your Organization and the World* (Boston: Harvard Business Press, 2009).
3. Mark E. Tidsworth, *Shift: Three Big Moves for the 21st Century Church* (Columbia, SC: Pinnacle Leadership Press, 2015).
4. Mark E. Tidsworth, *Farming Church: Cultivating Adaptive Change in Congregations* (Columbia, SC: Pinnacle Leadership Press, 2017).
5. Sunnie Giles, *How VUCA Is Reshaping the Business Environment, And What It Means for Innovation,* Forbes Online, May 9, 2018.
6. Tidsworth, *Shift.*
7. National Institute of General Medical Sciences, A Division of the National Institute of Health, An article entitled *Studying Genes* found at https://www.nigms.nih.gov/education/Documents/Studying_genes_final.pdf.
8. Two Sources: 1. Bible Study Tools, biblestudytools.com, *Kairos,* The New Testament Greek Lexicon. 2. Dictionary.com, Religion Section, *https://www.dictionary.com/e/religion/kairos/.*
9. It seems like this video was from early June, 2020, based out of a television news station in Fayetteville, NC. https://abc13.com/place/fayetteville/.

Chapter Two – Emerging Church Practice

1. Ecclesiastes 1:1-11 begins this book of wisdom with a rather bleak view of life. *"Vanity of vanities, says the Teacher, vanity of vanities! All is vanity,"* starts things off in verse one, followed by a description of the world by someone who just seems tired and bored. The writer seems to hold a deterministic point of view, not to mention a lack of expectation that much may come along. Verse nine is where this saying that's become fairly famous is found, *"What has been is what will be, and what has been done is what will be done; there is nothing new under the sun."*

2. *"If anyone boasts, "I love God," and goes right on hating his brother or sister, thinking nothing of it, he is a liar. If he won't love the person he can see, how can he love the God he can't see? The command we have from Christ is blunt: Loving God includes loving people. You've got to love both."* I John 4:20-21, The Message Version.
3. Find a chart entitled, *Phases Of Collective Trauma* Response by The Institute For Collective Trauma And Growth on their website here: https://www.ictg.org/phases-of-disaster-response.html.
4. Find another chart entitled, *The Emotional Life Cycle of a Disaster,* by Episcopal Relief & Development on their website here: https://www.episcopalrelief.org/wp-content/uploads/2019/07/emotional-lifecycle-of-a-disaster-copy.pdf.

Chapter Three – Reconnecting Church

1. For a straightforward description of Maslow's Hierarchy of Needs, see www.simplypsychology.org and do a search. You will find Maslow's diagram resembling a triangle and some explanation. Each need follows the one preceding it, assuming that one is met sufficiently. Beginning with the first, they are Physiological Needs, Safety Needs, Belongingness and Love Needs, Esteem Needs, and Self-actualization Needs.
2. Unity Presbyterian Church, Denver, NC...near Charlotte, NC. Rev. Dana Seiler is a Pinnacle Associate who is also the Associate Pastor at Unity. https://www.unitypres.org/ Thanks Dana for sharing this helpful Emerging Church Practice.
3. Rebecca Stead, *The List of Things That Will Not Change* (New York: Random House Children's Books, 2020).
4. G. Christopher Smith and John Pattison, *Slow Church: Cultivating Community in The Patient Way of Jesus* (Downers Grove, IL: Inter Varsity Press, 2014).

Chapter Four - Debriefing Our Experience

1. Jim Collins, *Good to Great* (New York: Harper Business, 2001). Pp.83-87.

Chapter Five – Sorting Our Progress

1. Malcolm O. Tolbert, *Commentary on Luke* (Nashville: Broadman Bible Commentary, 1970), pp.38-9.

Chapter Six – Choosing A Growth Mindset

1. Mary Oliver, *"The Summer Day"* in *New and Selected Poems* (Boston: Beacon Press, 1992).
2. Aldous Huxley, *Texts & Pretexts: An Anthology with Commentaries,* 1932.
3. Victor E. Frankl, *Recollections, An Autobiography* (New York: HarperCollins Publishers, 2000). This is one source of insight into Frankl's life. *Man's Search for Meaning* is another excellent book which is more about his worldview.
4. Carol S. Dweck, *Mindset: The New Psychology of Success* (New York: Ballentine Books, Random House Publishing, 2006). Read the entire book – it's excellent!

Chapter Eight – Aligning Our Structure

1. Thom S. Rainer and Eric Geiger, *Simple Church: Returning to God's Process for Making Disciples* (Nashville: B&H Publishing Group, 2007).
2. Rev. Dr. Eric Spivey, Pastor of First Baptist Church, Gainesville, FL. A big thanks to Eric for this phrase. Eric is an extremely creative pastor whose extreme love for people equips him with strong relational connection with the churches he serves so that they are willing to follow him into creative ministry. You might look in on FBC Gainesville periodically to see a traditional church faithfully engaging the emerging non-traditional culture emerging in its context.

Made in the USA
Columbia, SC
15 February 2022

55710427R00095